For One More Wish
A Journey Through Grief

Becky Cortesi-Caruso

Joshua Tree Publishing

• Chicago •

For One More Wish
A Journey Through Grief
Becky Cortesi-Caruso

Published by
Joshua Tree Publishing
• Chicago •
JoshuaTreePublishing.com

13-Digit ISBN: 978-1-956823-63-9
Front Cover Image Credit: Alex (Adobe Stock)

Disclaimer:
This book is designed to provide information about the subject matter covered. The opinions and information expressed in this book are those of the author, not the publisher. Every effort has been made to make this book as complete and as accurate as possible. However, there may be mistakes both typographical and in content. Therefore, this text should be used only as a general guide and not as the ultimate source of information. The author and publisher of this book shall have neither liability nor responsibility to any person or entity with respect to any loss or damage caused or alleged to be caused directly or indirectly by the information contained in this book.

Printed in the United States of America

Dedication

*To my beloved father, Robert Cortesi, thank you
for being my greatest teacher and best friend.
You left behind a legacy that will live on in me!*

*To those who are going through the grieving process,
please know that you are never alone.
I hope that this book will bring you comfort
through your journey.*

Table of Contents

Author's Note

Throughout my life, I've often heard the question, "What would you do if you were granted one wish?" I've always been fascinated by people's responses. What do you think most people would wish for? World peace? A loving family? Good health? Ending poverty? Surprisingly, many people express the desire to win the lottery and have all the money in the world.

This question has resonated with me for a very long time. Why do people wish for money? I could never imagine wishing for any amount of money to make me happy. I learned when I was younger that no amount of money could bring me happiness. In my humble opinion, our life experiences and our outlook on life define our happiness. Therefore, when I reflect back on my life, the only wish I would want is to spend one more day with my beloved father, who died over three decades ago.

My father was not just my best friend and mentor; he was an absolute inspiration to me. No amount of money in this world could match the happiness he brought me. Reflecting on this, I began thinking about the people closest to me: would they also choose to spend a day with a departed loved one if granted one wish?

For One More Wish explores not only my own personal narrative but also the narratives of those people who were courageous enough to write to me. It takes a great deal of transparency and courage to express the desire for one more day with the person you love most. The amazing people featured in this book authentically depict what their ideal day would entail.

Therefore, I ask you to read *For One More Wish* with an open mind and an honest heart. Imagine, if you had one day to spend with a departed loved one, what would it look like?

And so the story begins. *For One More Wish* is a story about the grieving process that all human beings go through. However, it is also about celebrating our loved one's legacy. It is about paying tribute to them while allowing ourselves to clearly transcend through the grieving process.

Chapter One

Wonder

As I sat in my car, waiting for my older daughter, I gazed outside the window and witnessed the most beautiful sunset illuminating the sky above the clouds. I found myself looking upward to see several rays of light streaming from the effervescent sky. What an awe-inspiring sight! Moments like these reminded me to stop and appreciate the small things in life.

As my daughter entered the car, she could tell by the wonder in my eyes that I had been in deep thought. She asked if I was all right. I told her I was fine. My daughter said, "Mom, what is on your mind?" My daughter, much like me when I was her age, was an old soul. There wasn't much I could keep from her. So I responded by posing a question to her: "If you had one wish to make in your life, what would it be?"

She talked incessantly about her dreams of becoming a famous actress and singing on Broadway. She continued to talk about all the famous people she would meet and how she was going to change the world. I sat quietly, listening to her. All I could think about was the beautiful life she had ahead of her and the positive impact she was going to make on the world! Her mannerisms and maturity were captured early in her life. While most young children were engrossed in playing with Barbie dolls and Legos, my daughter spent her time reading books beyond her age level and singing in her bedroom on most nights.

After she was done talking about what her future would look like, she asked me about my wish. I paused for a minute and simply responded, "If I could have one wish granted, it would be to spend one more day with my father."

"Aww, Mom, that is a beautiful wish," my daughter remarked.

Over the years, I have often wondered what that one day would look like if I could have my father back in my life. What would I say to him? What would we talk about? What would he think of me? Would he be proud of me? Would we pick up where we left off? Where would we be on our special day together? Was he finally at peace?

I've often found myself wondering what our time together would be like, imagining it in countless scenarios. While I might have initially thought I would have the entire day meticulously planned, the truth is, I would not have any specific plans at all.

I believe that *wonder* is a normal feeling for people who suffer through the death of a loved one. I wondered about what my life would have been like if my father had not died. To such an extent that life felt like it had stood still for me. Since my father's sudden death, I would often close my eyes to remember the last day I spoke to him. I relished in this last memory for a very long time until, eventually, it felt like a very distant memory.

Over the years, all three of my children have often wondered what it would have been like to know their grandfather. They have all asked how he died and why he was so young when he died. I never imagined in a million years having to relive the trauma that went along with his death. Just when I thought I had successfully gone through the grieving process, it hit me hard, stirring up emotions like a ton of bricks.

I could see the curiosity and wonder in the eyes of my children every time they asked me questions about their grandfather. As a former social worker, I knew that it was quite normal for my children to ask questions. However, I was traveling down uncharted emotional territory. I found myself doing my best to describe who my father was, but when it came to how he died, it was absolutely emotional to explain to my children that their grandfather died from a sudden heart attack.

I did my best to describe my father as a loving, hardworking, genuine, honest, and humble family man. I explained to my children that he dedicated his life to his family and his faith. He worked very hard to provide for those he loved. He was a gentle soul who was soft-spoken. He was the one I went to when I needed someone to listen to me without judgment. He sat quietly and listened without interruption. He offered positive advice and ultimately told me that there was nothing I could not achieve in this world. He would tell me to have confidence in myself and never second-guess my decisions. I have shared much of my father's advice with my own children. In essence, I could say that my father's legacy continues with my family!

One day, my older daughter asked me about what life was like growing up in my family. With a smile on my face, I told her that it was utter chaos. Despite the madness, my father would often sit quietly, wearing a grin. He tolerated quite a lot: three children, a variety of pets—four dogs, two cats, guinea pigs—and let's not forget my brother's lab rats. It was the positive memories that I focused on while talking to her. I explained to her that her grandfather was the epitome of a selfless human being who was always going out of his way for those around him. In turn, I explained to her that if he were alive today, he would have loved to attend her theater productions and listen to her beautiful voice.

What my daughter did not know was that her grandfather was one of the most well-rounded people I had ever met. He was a brilliant tradesman, crafting clocks for surrounding communities, repairing cars, showcasing his skills as a woodworker, and harboring a genuine love for the performing arts.

Toward the end of my father's life, he was working out of state and would come home every other weekend. It turned out to be the last conversation I would ever have with him. During our talk, he expressed surprise at how much I enjoyed attending theatrical and musical productions. He promised that when he returned home permanently from work, we would attend theater productions together.

I told my daughter when she was born, she was a true gift from my father; I explained that the odds of me having a girl were slim because we had so many boys in our family. I told her that I knew in my heart that she was our little blessing from an angel watching over us. Throughout the years, I have tried to keep my father's legacy alive by talking about him with my children. Most importantly, I want them to know how important he was in my life.

My daughter sat quietly as we finished our conversation with so much wonder in her eyes. She looked at me and said, "Mom, it must have been difficult for you to have your father die when you were a teenager."

I quietly responded, "Yes, it was awful. It changed my life forever. However, I like to think that my father's death gave me the courage and strength to go on with life."

I explained to her that I have always felt like I'm my dad's living legacy, continuing where he left off in life. In my heart, I know that is what he would have wanted for me.

Chapter Two

The Story of Us

I grew up in a traditional Italian family; our culture and faith were very important to our family. The importance of family was instilled in all of us at an early age. We had family meals together religiously every day of the week. Sundays were especially important because we attended church, participated in religious education, and enjoyed a lavish Italian feast for dinner. We spent the weekends with our extended family. From an early age, my parents taught us the importance of dedication to our faith and family and giving back to the world. My father's work ethic was beyond unreal, and the same went for my mother.

My father would leave for work before the sun came up, and he would return home between 5:00 p.m. and 6:30 p.m. He never complained and was a quiet man. He would come through the door, kiss my mom, ask her how her day was, and sit down for dinner. At dinnertime, he would ask each one of us about our day. He never asked for much from any of us. He was absolutely the best listener. He never had a bad word to say about anyone. He was the kindest and most gentle human being I had ever known.

I could never imagine what life would be like without him because he was such a permanent fixture in my everyday life. We shared a unique bond, a story that belonged solely to the two of us. Even from an early age, my father was my hero. When I was six years old, my mom would let me walk to the corner of the subdivision and wait for him to come home. I would walk by myself with my high heels and my purse and wait for him. Nowadays, I would never allow my children to leave my sight, but times were different back then. He would stop the car, pick me up on his lap, and let me drive home. He never complained, no matter how tired he was each day. He smiled at me, and we drove home. It was for those brief minutes in my life that we would talk about our day and spend time together.

There was a special feeling to being daddy's little girl; I was proud to say that I was his little girl. He wasn't just an ordinary dad; he was my best friend. Sadly, I never had the chance to tell him that he was the greatest inspiration in my life. I think that has been my biggest regret in life: never telling him how much I loved him and what an inspiration he was to me throughout my life. In short, I was so busy living my life that I forgot about his life. During most of my adolescent years, I rarely felt like I saw my father because of the long hours he worked. I went through a phase of self-absorption while my patient father watched me from afar.

Although my father worked long hours, he did his best to be physically present for me as my softball career began to intensify. My dad was there every step of the way. Despite lacking formal training and not being an athlete, he learned the game of softball and never left my side. He ensured that I received training from the best coaches available. He might not have been able to play the game, but he was an intelligent man who attentively listened to the coaches and understood the mechanics of pitching.

My love for the game stemmed from both of my parents' dedication and support in helping me achieve success. My mom was at every game, and my dad would come after work. However, it was not until my senior year of high school that the absence of my dad at my softball games truly hit me in a devastating way. There was a huge void in my life not having him during my last year of softball. He would no longer see the game we both grew to love. This was an incredibly challenging time in my life that I struggled to navigate as a young eighteen-year-old girl. The year that should have been the highlight of my life, sharing my softball journey with my father, never came to fruition. I was surrounded by wonderful friends and coaches who helped me through the most bittersweet year of my life. It was because of these people that I continued to play softball but on a much deeper level. While most athletes played to win, I played to survive the game of life.

Eventually, the news of my father's death spread around my small community. The stronger I became as a softball pitcher, the more attention I began to receive. I wasn't used to the attention, and frankly, it gave me anxiety. As I began to navigate this new way of living without my father, I found myself talking a lot about him with reporters when they called to talk to me about my softball career. Of course, they would compliment me on the great season I was having. However, shortly after the small talk, they would pose the million-dollar question: "How are you managing to excel on the pitching mound despite facing so much adversity in your young life?" So, I shared our story—a story about the love between a father and his daughter.

To this day, I believe my father's greatest gift to me was allowing me to continue to play the game I loved and giving me the strength to carry on. Playing softball wasn't just about playing a game; it was about surviving after tragedy and pulling myself out of a dark place in my life. Continuing to play softball allowed me to pay tribute to my father. I believe my story inspired other people who had suffered through their own grieving process. Shortly after my interviews, I began to receive letters from people thanking me for being transparent about my own journey and talking about their own grief.

Through it all, the one person who lifted me up when I was feeling depressed was my mom. She was a pillar of strength, almost to a fault, because I thought her way of grieving was the right way. You see, what we don't understand while we are going through the grieving process is that we watch our loved ones closely and the ways in which they grieve. We begin to compare ourselves to them. I began to ask myself why I was crying so much and could barely get through the day. Then, there was my mom getting up at 4:30 a.m. every day, going to work, and coming home to make dinner for us without complaining. I kept asking myself the following questions about the way my mom was grieving: Why wasn't she crying? Why wasn't she angry? Why wasn't she showing any type of emotion? Why doesn't she talk about my father? What is wrong with her, or is it me? Am I not grieving properly? These questions constantly consumed my mind.

It wasn't until several years later that my mom confided in me, revealing that she had many days when she cried herself to sleep. She felt really lonely, and yes, there were days when she could not get out of bed. She acknowledged how her life had drastically changed, but she lived for her children and knew she had to support us. She taught me the importance of living through adversity, even though she was hurting deeply inside. Although I did not see a lot of emotion from her, I knew she grieved in her own way.

Our journey through grief belongs to us. We are in control even when we think we are not. We find our own ways to grieve, but please remember to be authentic throughout this complicated process and remember to never forget your own special story with your loved one!

Chapter Three

Shock, Fear, Angst

The adolescence years are a time of being egocentric and not paying full attention to what is important in life. We are so consumed with trying to figure out who we are and where we belong that we overlook the needs of other people. At times in my life, I fit that description: not wanting to be with family, not wanting to talk to my parents, not wanting to spend quality time with them like we used to earlier on in my life. However, in the blink of an eye, my world was absolutely shattered into pieces, leaving me hopeless and alone. I could not even imagine picking up the pieces of my life and moving forward. My life had stopped, and the world around me was rapidly moving at a rate with which I could not keep up. The grief that I felt was inexplicable.

After my father's sudden death, I could not bring myself to leave my room, let alone my house. The absolute shock I had felt burning inside my body day after day did not go away for what seemed like an eternity. No matter what I tried to do in my life to get past the shock, nothing worked. Shock is a powerful feeling that truly cannot be explained until one experiences such trauma firsthand.

My once ordinary life changed forever. I was a typical teenager from a middle-class family with two parents who adored each other. But the family that I had once known had forever changed. Nothing could have prepared me for the devastation that suddenly erupted in our family. The insurmountable pain of grief was debilitating. Each day was a struggle to get out of bed and literally put one foot in front of the other. I used to be fearless, but suddenly, I began to fear everything. It felt like no one could understand what I was going through. Although people meant well, there were no words that they could express to me that made me feel better. Most of the time, I just tuned them out because I could not bear to listen to them. I was not trying to be rude; my mind just could not listen to anything being said to me. When your body goes into a state of shock, your mind goes into fight-or-flight mode. It becomes difficult to rationalize through your thoughts and emotions. Furthermore, it becomes an unbearable challenge to understand the trauma that has just transpired in your life and figure out how to pick up the pieces of your life and move forward.

My adolescence, as I knew it, was gone forever, and I matured quickly, burdened with worry. No matter how much my mom took care of all of us, I continued to worry. My mom tried her best to get me to lead a normal teenage life, but it never felt quite the same. Actually, I quickly learned that nothing in my life would be the same again because grief had a funny way of sneaking up behind me and knocking me right off my ass.

The constant fear was debilitating and hindered me from going out with friends for a long time. The lack of sleep and the fear that my mom might die in her sleep were constant. Many nights, I would go downstairs to check on her and make certain she was breathing. As a result, this constant worry kept me awake most nights, unable to sleep.

My darkest thoughts and fears plagued me during the late hours of the night as I tossed and turned in bed. The lack of sleep created major angst in me. This was the loneliest I had ever felt, and it was the time I dreaded the most because I knew I could not relax my brain enough to fall asleep. It was like I was living in a constant nightmare.

The sleep deprivation began to take a toll on my entire body. I began to battle through undiagnosed anxiety and depression for decades. I was not sure what was going on in my mind and body. I did not seek professional help. To be completely transparent, I was not raised in a family that spoke about mental health. The only coping mechanism I knew that worked for me (or so I thought it did) was keeping myself extremely busy. I tried never to have downtime because that is when my anxiety and depression would set in. However, I was desperate to figure out how to help myself because I was growing tired of always keeping myself busy. Here is some advice: you can only keep yourself busy for so long, and when you crash, you crash hard. The grief does not go away—it will linger like a bad apple.

I knew that I always enjoyed writing, so I thought to myself, why not try to begin writing some inspirational proverbs to help get me through my days? Writing was cathartic and therapeutic. It allowed me to express myself in ways I couldn't verbally with those around me. Then, one day, during my senior year, I encountered a mix of discomfort and familiarity as my world expanded slightly. It happened when the school social worker approached my mom and asked to speak with me. Despite my belief that my mom did not value the importance of mental health support, she gave her consent.

There I was, walking to the guidance office, not knowing why. If there was one thing anyone knew about me, it was that I did not like surprises! I remember sitting down for a brief second and then being greeted by a woman of small stature with a very calm voice. She smiled kindly at me and asked me to come to her office. My heart was racing, my body was sweating, and I nearly felt like I was going to pass out. I think she could sense that I was nervous and began to tell me that I was not in trouble. Instead, she explained that she was a social worker there to help students.

My first meeting with her was uncomfortable, to say the least. I had never visited a social worker before, and I felt a stigma attached to talking to her. Remember, I come from a family that did not discuss emotions or mental health openly. We did not seek help for emotional issues, nor did we talk about them.

The social worker could sense my angst, so she pulled out a stack of Uno cards and asked me if I wanted to play. I remember thinking that this lady had the best job in the world! While we played Uno, she asked me how I was doing and if there was anything that she could do to support me. I did not want to be disrespectful, but in my mind, I was thinking to myself, *How do you seriously think I am doing? My father died a week ago. I feel like shit. I don't want to be in school, and my life has just been turned upside down. Oh, and one more thing to mention—I feel like I am living in a nightmare of a movie where the world is moving mega fast, and I am drowning in a sea of shit!*

Of course, I would never say any of that to a social worker. I remained compliant while answering her questions and did my best not to reveal how uncomfortable I truly felt during our brief time together. However, I found myself asking her questions about herself and her job. This would be called "deflection." You see, I was not ready to talk about my father's death. It had only been a week since his death, and honestly, every day was an absolute struggle to get through. It was easier for me to focus on her career and how she got students to open up to her.

I must admit that seeing her was not an absolute loss, as I found her job intriguing. This sparked my interest in the field of social work. In the short time I spent with her, she actually inspired me!

For the next year, my perfectionistic self would keep busy with school, softball, writing, and researching colleges for social work. Who knew that one visit to the school social worker would change my life! Over the years, I have often thought about her and wondered if she remembered me or realized the impact she had on my life. What I learned from her soft-spoken demeanor and zen-like personality was that it only takes one stranger in my life to make one awkward moment extremely memorable.

Chapter Four

Stages of Grief

I s there such a thing as good grief? I have asked myself this question a million times. What is the difference between bad grief and good grief? As I grew older, I learned a lot about the grieving process. To this day, I wish someone had taught me earlier in my grieving process about the importance of understanding the five stages of grief.

Besides my father dying, transcending through the grieving process was the most challenging time in my life. As an adolescent, I did not know anything about the stages of grief, nor did I have anyone to help guide me through this process. Were my feelings normal? Why did I feel so confused? Why was I bargaining with God? Why was I so angry? Why did I push the people I loved the most out of my life? There were so many unanswered questions. The only way I could begin to answer these questions was through self-education and by discerning the difference between what I called good grief and bad grief.

While researching the grieving process, I learned about Dr. Elisabeth Kübler-Ross, a psychiatrist and a pioneer in the field of death and dying studies. Dr. Ross was an expert in educating people on the five stages of grief. She dedicated her life to researching and understanding the complexities of the grieving process.

Dr. Elisabeth Kübler-Ross's explanation of the grieving process had a profound impact on my life. It was the first time I truly understood the feelings I was going through, and the raw emotions that permeated throughout my body were all part of the grieving process. For the first time in a decade, I felt like I was not going crazy. There was a process I could now educate myself on.

Understanding the grieving process allowed me to comprehend my own journey. The grieving process is like a roller coaster: you never know what each day is going to look like for you. In the early stages of grief, every day is an absolute struggle. It is a struggle to get up, a struggle to take a breath, a struggle to put one foot in front of the other, a struggle to talk to anyone, and an overall struggle to accept the death of the loved one. In short, you feel like you are trying to wake up from a never-ending nightmare.

My life felt like it was going in slow motion while others my age continued on with their lives. The best analogy I could share with anyone who is going through the beginning stages of grief is to imagine yourself frozen in time as everything and everyone around you is moving at the speed of light. Is this feeling normal? Yes, yes, it is!

I didn't know many kids my age who had experienced the death of a parent, so I felt alone in it. I did not know how to grieve, let alone understand the difference between bad grief and good grief. As I began reading books related to death and dying, I began to understand the importance of embracing all of my feelings. I cried when I wanted to cry, and I didn't apologize for it. I screamed when I wanted to without regret, and at times, I gave myself permission to laugh. I knew that expressing all of these mixed emotions was my way and a healthy way to grieve. These were all signs of good grief.

Most of us going through the grieving process do not understand where to turn after the death. Our minds are not clear, and our hearts are broken—so much so that we fall into a deep state of denial about our loved one's passing.

Denial is the first stage of the grieving process, and it took me some time to realize that I was stuck in this stage. I learned, after a specific period of time, that it was acceptable for me to be in this stage. I learned that everyone experiences denial when someone they love dies. So, what does this stage look like? Denial can manifest differently for each person. The intriguing aspect of the grieving process is that each individual's experience is unique to them. I can only speak to my own journey through the grieving process, hoping that it may offer some insights to others going through their own.

I watched the front door, hoping my father would walk through it. I would pick up the phone to call him, only to remember there was no one to call. It took several months for me to finally accept that he would not walk through the door or call me. I remember being on the softball field, yearning to see him behind the backstop one more time. Sometimes, I even visualized him quietly standing there, motioning to me on how to correct my form. He used to do that often at my games, which used to annoy me, but oh, how I wished he was still there with me.

Denial is real and a very difficult stage to overcome, and it's challenging to truly understand because of the magnitude of the shock that one faces when someone dies. The brain is trained to protect us from the pain that we experience in life, so denial sets in until we are ready to face our new reality.

Eventually, I came to terms with not seeing my father and slowly found ways to move forward with my life. Although my life had been forever changed, I knew I had to carry on. So, that is exactly what I did: I slowly found ways to live without the presence of my father. However, no one could prepare me for the anger that would begin to settle into my daily life.

Anger is the second stage of grief. This stage of grief was one of the worst for me. Simply put, I was absolutely pissed off at the world. I was so angry that my father died at the age of forty-four. The day I found out the news of his death, my life literally passed before me. It was like taking a video recorder and putting it in fast forward, and my life flashed right before me without him. He would never see me graduate from high school or college. He would not be there as I signed my letter of intent for a full Division One Softball Scholarship. He would never be there to see me accept my first job, walk me down the aisle, or share in the miracle of me being the mother to three beautiful children. He would never celebrate any monumental moments in my life. I would never be able to listen to his wisdom and advice again.

The insurmountable anger that existed deep down within my soul was unbearable. The reality of my life had forever changed, yet I had to find a way to deal with my anger because I was stuck in a state of "bad grief" that consumed me. I sabotaged all my relationships with men, fearing they would leave me or die. I was not always the best friend to my friends. I harbored a constant fear of abandonment and could not handle any more loss in my life. In short, I spent many years reflecting on why I was angry and how I could become a better human being because I disliked who I was becoming.

People release their anger differently: some are mad at the world, some engage in physical altercations, some self-medicate using drugs and alcohol, and some lose their faith along the way. Unfortunately for me, I lost my faith along the way. I questioned God for taking my father so young. I had so many questions for God; to this day, some remain unanswered, while I've answered others myself in order to cope with my personal loss.

I learned along the way that it's all right to question God; it is a natural thing to do. However, at some point in the grieving process, you have to let go and accept the fact that sometimes, bad things happen to good people for no apparent reason. I will never understand why my beloved father was taken from this world, but after so many years of asking, I realized it was time to stop.

As humans, we are meant to feel an array of emotions. However, it can be difficult to cope with so many emotions at once, especially when someone we love dies. The human heart has its limits, and what we often overlook is how the heart and mind can play tricks on us during the grieving process. For instance, think about the word "bargaining." We know it as a word that means "to negotiate." However, during the five stages of grief, it appears and feels differently to those experiencing the grieving process.

Bargaining is the third stage of grief and can be quite complicated. We begin to question and negotiate the "what if" or "should have." We begin to negotiate with ourselves and/or God.

"What if I go back to church and regain my faith? Will that be enough to bring my loved one back?"

"If only I had treated him better, he would not have suddenly died."

"If I had not wished her dead, would she still be alive?"

"Why didn't I make him go to the doctor?"

"If I had driven by his house to check on him, would he still be alive?"

As I mentioned before, the mind and heart play tricks on us. The bargaining stage is overwhelming to go through because the survivor second-guesses everything in the past that they possibly should have done or should have said to the loved one. The survivor goes through a sense of guilt during the bargaining stage. Furthermore, the survivor needs to understand that there was nothing they did or said that caused the death of their loved one.

I can personally attest to the experience of going through this stage. Recently, I reconnected with a former colleague of mine. We used to work together over two decades ago, but we always checked in on each other. One night, he texted me, asking me if I wanted to meet him at the local bar. I told him that I was sick with COVID. He replied, "No worries, we will connect soon." Soon after that text, I was reading his suicide note on Facebook. As I read the note, my heart sank, and I literally felt sick to my stomach. I immediately called the authorities, but they had been notified by many people and were already out looking for my friend. I began to pace back and forth in my home, and then I was ready to leave the house to go find him when my husband intervened. In short, he prevented me from going out to search for my friend that night.

For months afterward, I could not shake the feeling of what might have happened if I had met him at the bar that night. No matter how much training I had as a former therapist and social worker, I could not stop bargaining with myself. It wasn't until one of my beloved friends called me and simply said, "Becky, I am worried about you. Are you doing all right?"

It was at this moment that I knew that I had to let go, but it was not easy. To this day, my heart goes out to his daughter and his entire family. He had a heart of gold, and he will always be remembered for his larger-than-life personality.

Once reality sets in and the survivor finally realizes that no amount of bargaining can bring their loved one back, they may spiral into depression. Honestly, the stage of depression is a ruthless and exhausting stage to go through, especially if you don't have the right support in place or if you do have the support but push them away.

Depression is the fourth stage of the grieving process, and it can take over your life in a matter of seconds without you even realizing it. It almost sneaks up on you, and before you know it, it kicks your ass.

For many years, I didn't even know the effects that depression had physically on my body. I would complain of major body aches, headaches, and numbness in my limbs. Then, one day, I ended up in the emergency room, feeling like I was having a heart attack. It would take years before I realized that all of my symptoms were brought on by the way I was feeling and/or the fear that I experienced after my father's death.

Many symptoms I experienced throughout my life were related to the death of my father. The anxiety, chest pains, shortness of breath, difficulty swallowing, and numbness throughout my body felt very real to me. However, it was not until I began studying for my Masters in Social Work that I realized I had been exhibiting psychosomatic symptoms throughout my grieving process.

You might wonder what psychosomatic symptoms are. They are symptoms caused by your mind when your body is under stress. You might experience headaches, stomach aches, heart palpitations, shortness of breath, and overall body achiness. These feelings are real and are brought on by a person's emotional state. Just like any other medical condition, it is very important to seek medical attention to rule out any underlying issues.

My studies in the field of social work ultimately helped me with the rest of my grieving process. Yes, I had really bad days of feeling depressed, but I became more educated and better equipped to cope with my depression. I began exploring positive ways to deal with my grief, also known as "good grief." I began writing a lot of inspirational proverbs each day to keep my spirits high. In addition, I had always been an athlete, so I stayed active to help heal my body. Eventually, I began praying at night to my dad and God to assist me throughout my grieving process.

My best advice for anyone struggling with depression is to never lose sight of what you are passionate about in life and continue doing it. I have always admired people who are artistically talented or musically inclined because both are awesome forms of therapy. Someone very close to me who was diagnosed with major anxiety and depression once said that performing on stage was a release from her everyday life.

She explained, "I have lived with depression and anxiety since middle school. As a young adult, when I get on stage to perform, my anxiety and depression are drowned out by the adrenaline of the performance. Although I try to be the best version of myself, acting is an escape. I won't lie—my anxiety does not go away, but for a brief moment, performing as a character or singing a song helps me cope with any challenging emotions in my everyday life. Each production allows me to enter into another realm and pushes me to exceed my limits. When I feel the dark walls of anxiety and depression caving in on me, I go to a practice room on my college campus and sing. But before I sing, I practice coping skills: deep breathing exercises, relaxation strategies, and positive self-talk. I have always been my worst critic, so it is important for me to reflect on my ability to cope with my mental health. Most importantly, I have stopped mourning the fact that I am not perfect and that I struggle every day with thoughts of anxiety and depression. I am proud that I can acknowledge that I am a survivor and that I channel my emotions through the performing arts."

I promise to those of you reading this book that there is a light at the end of the tunnel! There is no magic wand available when going through the grieving process, and there is definitely no timeline. However, the true healing phase begins when a person reaches the acceptance stage of grief.

Finding *acceptance* in your heart after the death of a loved one is the fifth stage of grief.

I have always explained to people that the healing process begins when they can accept the fact that their loved one is not returning to the physical world. However, we must always celebrate the memories we have with our loved ones to get through our days. I have never told anyone that in time, it will get easier to cope with the loss. On the contrary, I have said that as we learn to live life again, we find new ways to heal our mind, body, and soul.

Acceptance of death doesn't mean forgetting about your loved one; it means finding a place in your heart to move forward in life as your loved one would have wanted you to. I honestly can't tell you when I came to a place of acceptance about my father's death. I know I did not wake up one day and say, "I accept that you're never coming back to this world." I believe it took me decades to come to terms with it.

Through it all, I have lived, loved, lost, and become a much stronger and wiser human being than I could have imagined. This is my advice for all of you going through your own grieving process: don't be afraid to live without regret, love to your fullest potential, and understand that part of living is understanding that, at some point, we all go through the grieving process.

Chapter Five

Life After Loss

Real life resumes, and we are forced to pick up the pieces of our lives and figure out how to live without our loved one. I admit this is one of the most difficult parts of living after the death of a loved one. I often found myself wanting to ask those around me to slow down, take a break, talk a little slower, or try to understand how difficult it was for me to take a breath.

As I reflected on how others were living their lives, it brought back all of my own memories—memories that I wanted to relive over and over because they were with my father. Sometimes, I felt like I was stuck in time, searching for normalcy. I missed my fast-paced life. However, I realized I never slowed down to appreciate the finer moments. It was not until after my father died that I realized I had not captured many of our memories; I did not have any photographs of him, nor did I have many of us together. I am not one to live with regret, but man, this was one of my biggest regrets, and the realization set in that my father would eventually become a distant memory to me.

Life after the death of a loved one made me feel differently; I felt like a shell of myself. The typical teenage life that I had once known was no longer. I felt that people were treating me differently. There were those who were there for me after the death and those who slowly faded away. I believe those people who faded out of my life did so because of the discomfort they felt. I learned years later that it had nothing to do with me but more about them. They did not know what to say or do for me, so it was easier to fade away. Most people in my life meant well, but they wanted me to return to my normal way of life. Honestly, there was nothing normal about my life anymore.

Life after the death of a loved one is like a chaotic storm that rips through a family and shatters each one of them into tiny pieces. At least, this was my experience with my own family. The death of the loved one takes a different toll on each family member, and the way they cope with the grieving process looks different. For me, the death of my father consumed me to the point that it hurt to take a physical breath and to live. It would be the people who stayed with me after the death that would help me gain my strength. They were there through some of my darkest hours, but most importantly, they sat with me in silence. They understood that the best form of friendship that I needed was not judgment, not conversation, but just being physically present in my life and allowing me to grieve in silence.

My ability to grieve in silence allowed me to be physically present in the moment with no expectations placed upon me. Grieving in silence lets you reflect on the agony you feel but also allows you to channel this intrinsic emotion that permeates your body. At times, when my anxiety was under control, I tried to meditate to bring harmony to my mind, body, and soul. In short, I found that grieving in silence allowed me to get my body and mind into a calm state.

There is a calm that our loved ones bring to the grieving family in the days leading up to the memorial services. The pain and angst that go along with waiting for the memorial services are never-ending. So many emotions surge through your entire body as you wait to view the body of someone you love more than life itself. My grandfather tried to prepare me for the viewing of my father, but can anyone ever be fully prepared? The answer is no.

Approaching the casket, I took a deep breath, and tears began rolling down my face. What were the chances that my tears would hit my father's face just right and smear his makeup? My grandfather panicked and said, "Becca, it's okay." He tried to pull me away from the casket, but I refused to leave. I told him it was fine and proceeded to fix my father's makeup. Let's just say I really messed up his makeup. Part of me was freaking out, but then, out of nowhere, I began laughing. I think my family was mortified because all I could do was laugh. Eventually, his makeup was fixed, and we went about that very long day.

I was only eighteen when my father died, and I had no idea what I was in for leading up to the services. Looking back, I can find humor in the stupid comments people made about a dead person. At the time, I found myself speechless with all the stupidity that surrounded me. Standing at the foot of the casket, I felt like a shell of myself while people came up to me and hugged me.

Number one, the last place I wanted to be was at the memorial service, and number two, I literally cringed when someone hugged me. It was an emotionally exhausting and uncomfortable few days. Then, after everything was over, the realization and pain set in that my father was gone forever. The yearning for a loved one is so painful that living after the loss becomes somewhat of a psychological game.

Each day, I had to convince myself to get out of bed, get into the shower, and attend school. Once I entered school, I had to visualize what my day was going to look like and then begin to use positive self-talk to get me through the day. It was not uncommon for me to walk down the halls and in my head state the following: "You got this, Becky. Just try to focus." The only comfort I had on a given day was seeing my mom at the high school I attended. She would always smile while serving me lunch, and she was an absolute comfort to see every day. She always reminded me that life goes on and that we have to make the best of terrible situations.

The moral of my story is that I wrote my own narrative; I survived a great loss in my life and lived to tell about it. I promised myself decades ago that I would tell my story in the hope that I could help those who were also grieving.

Life after loss is not easy; it is a journey—a journey that only you can go through. Never let the memories fade; never lose sight of what is important to you! Always remember your loved ones and be brave enough to write your own narrative!

Chapter Six

One More Day

My greatest wish has always been to spend one more day with my beloved father. Countless times in my life, I've yearned for the chance to spend a day with him and catch up on the many life events he missed.

Questions raced through my mind: What would I say to him? What would he say to me? What would we talk about? Was he proud of me?

At different stages in my life, I would go outside, lie on the grass, and stare at the million stars in the sky, wishing for one more day with my beloved father. On one particular night, I closed my eyes and took a deep breath, drifting off into a calm state of peace and quiet. My mind wandered to thoughts of my father and whether he thought of me and sent me signs that he was with me in spirit. Suddenly, I smelled a familiar fragrance—Old Spice. I was not dreaming! My wish had come true! He was here with me on my one special day—a day I will never forget.

As I walked, I noticed a distant shadow ahead of me. Drawing nearer, I discerned a man wearing a teal-and-gray sweatshirt standing behind a softball backstop. The very same backstop where he used to stand while I pitched! It brought back memories of the umpire asking him to step away because he distracted me. Despite the years that had passed, there he was, in the exact spot I remembered him.

As tears rolled down my face, I gave him a huge hug and did not want to let go. He hugged me with all his strength and said how much he had missed me. We cried together, and for that one moment, my one wish had come true: I was reunited for one more day with my best friend, my father!

Sitting on the bleachers, we began to talk about life. I talked a mile a minute, but my dad calmly said, "Becky, slow down. We have all day." He quietly asked how I had been since his death. With tears in my eyes, I simply replied, "There has not been a day that has gone by that I haven't thought of you." He smiled and said, "I know you have, Becky. You are an amazing and strong woman!"

As I began to talk about his sudden loss and its impact on me, I began to choke up. Decades of emotions seemed to flood over me. I found myself gasping for air. My heart raced, and my throat felt like it was closing up.

My father put his arm around my shoulder and said, "Becky, it's all right. Take a deep breath. Sometimes, bad things happen to good people. We can't undo what's done. We have to find ways to move forward, and that's all I ever wanted for all of you. My life might have been cut short, but I left behind a beautiful family. Take you, for instance. You've carried on where I left off! I've watched you from above, dedicating your life to those less fortunate. You've used your knowledge and passion to better the lives of others. What more could I ask of you?" As I listened to his wise words, I smiled through tears. What a moment!

As I began to talk about my senior year in high school, I could see the pain in his eyes. I asked him if he was all right. My father stated, "I was not ready to leave this earth. I had so much more to do for my family. I'm so sorry I wasn't there for you." His eyes held genuine pain, and I could feel the angst in his heart. It was the most difficult conversation to have with him.

He continued, "Becky, I could see you. I know I wasn't physically there for you, but I could see you! I was with you on the softball field before every game. I heard your prayers as you looked up to the sky, wishing that I was there every step of the way. I was there on the days when you wanted to give up, and I was there to celebrate when you played your heart out on the field. Most importantly, I was there with you when you signed your letter of intent to play softball at a Division One university! Oh, how proud I was of you! A dream you had since you were a little girl, you made it a reality! I want you to know that I heard you in your darkest moments, and I never left your side!"

The next phase of my life was going away to college, where I was on my own for the first time. I won't lie; I was scared beyond belief. There was so much uncertainty in my life. "Dad, I didn't deal with the finality of your death, and here I was, four and a half hours from home all by myself with the pressures of playing softball and keeping my grades up. I had the weight of the world on my shoulders, knowing that my college tuition was paid in full but also acknowledging that I was not the same person emotionally and physically."

I remember my dad sitting quietly as we spoke about some of my hardships. He smiled and stated, "You did the unthinkable, Becky! You dedicated your heart and soul to playing the game of softball and being an excellent student-athlete. What more could you ask of yourself? Life throws you curveballs, no pun intended." I always laughed at his quirky jokes and his witty personality. My dad was the only person who had a calming impact on me.

Life did throw me some crazy curveballs! Right before my freshman year of college, I was in a serious car accident that made my life flash before my eyes. It forever changed my life. So, my first year of college was not a typical year for me. But then again, nothing about my life felt typical after my father's death. I soon realized that being far from my family was not what I wanted. Shortly after, I transferred home to be closer to my mom and to gain insight into helping myself on an emotional level.

My dad said, "Sometimes, unfortunate circumstances in our lives make us think about what is important to us. The car accident gave you clarity in your life. It's all right for you to have followed a dream and realize that maybe this is not what you wanted, or maybe timing was not on your side."

There were many moments in my life when I felt that time was not on my side, a struggle that felt so real for me. However, I learned that if I kept persevering through the difficult moments in my life, I would become stronger and wiser about how to handle such struggles. This was a conversation that I had yearned for with my beloved father.

We strolled across the softball field just like we used to when I was a child, chatting and reminiscing without a care in the world. He expressed how proud he was of me and how he never worried about me after he left this earth. He knew I would be all right. He grabbed my hand and firmly held it, and with tears in his eyes, he said, "Becky, you have made me so proud of the person you have become. You have worked so hard to build a life of service—service to those less fortunate. You set out to do everything that we had spoken about. All a father could ever want for their child is someone who gives back to the world, and that is what you have accomplished."

I talked incessantly about my work as a school social worker and how proud I was of the students and families that I had worked with throughout the years. Being a school social worker was a challenging career but could also be very rewarding. My dad sat and listened to me, smiling with every word, almost like he was relishing in my stories.

We spoke a lot about love and loss and the impact it had on me. It was very difficult for me to see my dad be so vulnerable. I could see in his eyes how disheartened he was that he could not be there for me when I went through my breakups. As much as I tried to have successful relationships, I always found a way to sabotage them. It was easier to be the one to end a relationship rather than be hurt by the person I was dating.

My dad stated, "Becky, love and loss are two of the hardest emotions to feel, but you lived through all of it and emerged stronger." He went on to tell me that my mom was the love of his life. There was no one that he would have rather been with in this lifetime. At that point, I could feel the pain in his heart. He said, "With every great life lived, there is ultimately loss. However, there is always a silver lining. I was able to love your mom from the age of sixteen to the day that I died. What more could I ask for? Of course, I wish every day we could have celebrated our twenty-fifth wedding anniversary, but the reality is that it didn't happen."

He went on to talk about love and loss, and in those brief minutes of our conversation, I learned more than I could have imagined by listening to his wisdom. My father said, "Remember, love is precious, love is kind, love shall not hurt, but rather bring out the best in you. Even when you go through challenging times, never give up. Always find the silver lining."

"Find the silver lining"—a motto I would live by for the rest of my life.

I told my dad that his wisdom would guide me throughout the rest of my life. I found the silver lining in meeting the love of my life and my best friend. I believe that meeting my husband, Mike, was a gift from my dad. I told my dad that Mike loved me for me and understood that there was nothing easy that came along with being with me. Mike tolerated my ups and downs. Even though Mike was not the best communicator, I knew he cared deeply for me. He gave me the time I needed on my bad days and did not ask questions. But I knew that if I needed him, he would be there for me.

My dad smiled as I spoke about Mike, almost like he already knew him. I described our relationship and emphasized how much he meant to me. I told him that Mike had proposed to me within six months of getting to know me and that we had planned to marry twelve months later. My dad grabbed my hand and said, "I know you are in good hands, and I know that he loves you dearly. You have something extraordinary because he was your friend first!"

I went on to tell my dad about my wedding day, the most difficult day of my life next to the day he died. It was very difficult to explain all of the emotions I was feeling on both of those days. The day my father died, a piece of me died with him. The day I married my husband was the most bittersweet day of my life because my father, who had always been my best friend, would not be there to walk me down the aisle.

I told my dad that I was proud of myself because I didn't cry that much! I woke up early and went for a long run where

I could reflect on the day. While running, I felt at peace with the day and told myself that I was going to get through this day because I knew he would have wanted that for me.

Then, something absolutely amazing happened to me. One of my bridesmaids delivered a letter from one of my closest friends. He wrote a beautiful letter saying how proud he was of me and how proud my dad would have been of me. His letter gave me the hope, love, and strength that I needed to make it through my wedding day. To this day, he will always be my best friend!

During this conversation, my dad's eyes welled up with tears. He said, "I am heartbroken that I was not there to walk you down the aisle, to say how much I loved you, and to express to you how breathtaking you looked on that day. There was nothing more I could have ever wanted than to walk you down the aisle."

It has been decades since my dad's death; however, it feels like yesterday. I told him that I had found ways to cope with his death. However, the trauma of his death never went away.

The day I found out that my father had died was as vivid in my head as anything that I have ever experienced. The feelings began to resonate with me more and more when I began having my own children. As they grew older, they had a million questions for me about my dad.

My dad and I spoke about my three beautiful children and how these amazing kids saved my life. They gave me purpose to live not just an ordinary life but an extraordinary one. As I spoke about each one of them, my dad cried. He shed tears of both joy and sadness. I told him that I never imagined how much I would need him on this journey we call "parenthood."

I needed his calm disposition to guide me through the good and bad times of parenting three children with three different personalities. He stopped me while I was in mid-sentence and said, "You don't need my help; you are doing just fine. Part of being a parent is taking the good and the bad, making sure your children know that they are loved even through the most challenging times in their lives. Becky, we are human, and we make mistakes along the way. As long as you can teach your children to live authentically, love unconditionally, and laugh often, you are doing all right in my book!"

As our day was coming to a close, I won't lie—I was filled with emotion. I could feel the tightness in my chest, the angst in my body, and the tears building up in my eyes. My dad put his arms around me, hugged me as tight as he could, and said, "I will cherish this day forever. Even though I'm not with you physically in this world, I will always be here in spirit!"

He continued to say, "Promise me that you will look past your pain and continue to make a difference in this world. Please continue on where I left off and be my living legacy! Mend your broken heart for me and share the rest of it with Mike and your beautiful children. Remember what is important to you, and don't lose sight of it. Live your life authentically, love unconditionally, and promise me that you will laugh often! I will love you with all of my heart, and thank you for making me proud of the person you have become!"

Chapter Seven

The Day After

I could never imagine how I would feel the day after seeing my father. I had to take time to digest the beautiful day we had together. I felt a sense of calmness come over me, which I had not felt in years. I finally had the closure that I needed after decades of grieving. I played that day over and over in my head so that I would never forget it. I hung on to his every word. He had a way of always knowing the right words to say to me. He exuded a sense of calmness throughout our day together. Maybe he had experienced the same sense of closure that I had that day.

The conversation we had helped me to reevaluate my priorities and consider what truly mattered to me. For a very long time, I had led a fast-paced life, striving to secure the best job and maximize my earnings. I was driven by my career and money, although I didn't boast about my possessions. It was a certain lifestyle that drove me, one that eventually didn't hold as much importance for me.

I learned through my dad that there was no amount of money that could bring happiness. I will never forget what he told me. He said, "Becky, don't listen to anyone who tells you that money brings them happiness. True happiness does not come from money. It comes from living a decent and honest life." This was coming from a man who never got to see all the money he left behind when he died.

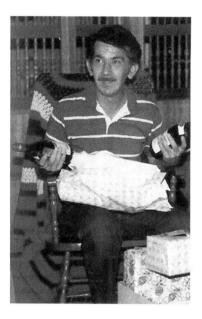

On our special day together, I had never seen him so at peace with himself. He had this effervescent glow to him. I never recalled my dad having that look while he was alive. I remembered a run-down, tired man who always seemed preoccupied. Although he was gone from the physical world, he seemed to be in a much better place, free from the stress of his previous life.

Reflecting on my father's life, I started to plan a new journey for my own. I began to understand that my happiness depends on me and no one else and that no amount of money or materialistic things can overshadow my intrinsic happiness.

Chapter Eight

Celebrating Our Loved Ones

I began thinking about those special people around me who have suffered loss in their own lives. If they were given one wish, would they also ask to spend one last day with a departed loved one? It was a slippery slope because I had to acknowledge that not everyone thought like me. However, I wanted to give people an opportunity to imagine what one last day could look like for them and their loved ones. After a loss, it's common to bury our feelings deep down within us and never talk about our loved one. Therefore, this was my way to encourage them to remember that special person and celebrate that day.

So, I ask you: if you had one more day with your loved one, how would you feel? From the moment you saw that person, what feelings would arise within your body? What would your first response be? What do you think your loved one would say? Where would you be? How would you spend that one special day?

As we ponder these questions, we begin to have one more day with our loved one—not only to remember them but also to celebrate their lives while bringing closure for ourselves. No one day looks the same for people, which is why I believe the idea of having one more day with our loved one is so special!

If each of us had the ability to imagine what one more day would look like, our stories would look different. Our perspective on the grieving process might even vary. Therefore, the death of a loved one impacts each human being differently. However, it is important to celebrate how their lives impacted the world!

So, I encourage people around me to imagine what their day would be like if they had one more chance to spend with a loved one who has passed away. As I began reading the emails sent to me, a common theme emerged. People began conversing with their departed loved ones about their lives and how much they missed them. They reminisced about cherished memories and celebrated the life of the person who died. Every story told is a life remembered by each of these people and a journey never to be forgotten.

The following stories were shared by people of different backgrounds, each detailing how they would spend their day. The remarkable uniqueness of each narrative was absolutely amazing to read. As I crafted a chapter dedicated to each person's story, I began to understand the vulnerability and deep love that exist between them and their departed loved ones. What unites us all is our willingness to embrace vulnerability and share stories near and dear to our hearts, keeping the legacy of our loved ones alive!

Chapter Nine

To Know Her Better

In my life, there have been perfect strangers who helped me through challenging times. What's incredible is that a few of these perfect strangers became close confidants. Rikk Dulap became one of those people.

Rikk is an amazing and talented writer whose manuscript became a Hallmark movie. His movie entitled *Christmas Under the Stars* became one of my favorite movies, and Rikk became one of my favorite friends. Rikk is one of the kindest people that I know and has a heart of gold. He is empathetic, intuitive, and intelligent. When I faced defeat in my writing or encountered imposter syndrome, Rikk was just a phone call away to lift me up when I was down. So, it was only natural for me to ask Rikk to contribute to this book. While Rikk has his own story to tell, for the purpose of this book, he has chosen to write about his beloved sister, who tragically passed away at a young age.

***

Kristin was my younger sister, the youngest of the two sisters in our family. As a child, she was a skinny, energetic little heartbreaker with an infectious smile and a magnetic personality that drew people close to her. She eagerly sought to be involved in whatever activities others were doing, particularly enjoying adventurous pursuits.

She married in her twenties, but starting a family came with complications. Not one to give up easily, she persisted, and in time, my sister became a mother. Four more children followed in quick succession, her last two being twins. Kristin wasn't just a mom by title. She took part in her kids' lives, encouraged their creativity and talents, and bragged about their accomplishments with a mother's pride. By all appearances, she had made a good life for herself and her family. So it seemed.

As her kids grew and the older ones left home to start lives of their own, cracks weakened her already unstable foundation. She sought attention from anyone who offered it to her. Unfortunately, it was given by the wrong people, and she fell into a cavern of addiction and behavior that drove away those of us who truly loved her. She'd fooled herself into believing her secret was neatly hidden and that she had it all under control.

I've been sober for over thirty years, and I know the addict's mind. I know all the lies and deceptions because I'd used them myself. From the beginning, I haven't kept my drinking problem a secret. Instead, I use my recovery to help others. My primary focus has always been high school students. As a professional speaker, I've shared my story with thousands. As a brother, I reached out to my sister. Her response was the same lies and deception I had used in the past. She wasn't ready.

Circumstances with Kristin grew worse, and she slipped away a little at a time. Those were her darkest days. Talking to her did no good. All we could do was watch and pray. Then, somehow, she managed to regain herself and turn her life around. Perhaps it was the birth of her third grandchild. A new life and a fresh hope. Whatever it was, it felt good to have her back with us. Her middle daughter was married on a beautiful October afternoon. Kristin looked better than I had seen her in years. She smiled again, laughed, and seemed more like her old self. She looked genuinely happy, surrounded by her children and her growing family. It was the last time I would ever see my sister alive.

Some people routinely tempt fate. They deal the cards, throw their chips in the pot, and poker-face their way through with a less-than-winning hand. Eventually, fate tires of the game, calls their bluff, cleans them out, and leaves the table. Then, there are those who don't know when they're beat. They call fate out for one more hand. Winner takes all. It's never a good idea.

COVID had just spread across the globe, scaring everyone into their homes and away from loved ones. As a family, we decided to skip our Thanksgiving dinner together. Two weeks later, my mom called me at work. I'd never heard that kind of panic in her voice. Something bad had happened. She kept saying that they couldn't wake Kristin up. I asked her what that meant. She said, "Kristin is gone."

On the drive to my mom's house, I mentally prepared myself for what was waiting. Everyone would be there. I put my grief aside in order to comfort my family. It had been exactly one year since my dad had passed away. How were we going to handle another loss so quickly? We gathered in my mom's living room and pieced together the final hours of my sister's life. Two of her daughters had found her slumped over on the bed. She'd died alone in her bedroom with the door closed sometime in the night, yet she wasn't discovered until the following morning. A small bag with white residue lay next to her face. The police immediately turned the home into a crime scene. Toxicology reports later confirmed what we already knew. Drug overdose. Fentanyl.

Nothing made sense. She was excited about Christmas, which was only days away, and had big plans for the coming year. She began mending relationships and had such a positive outlook. So why did this happen? That is a question we can't answer. To the best of my ability, I helped my family understand the disease of addiction, hoping to give them some glimmer of reasoning over Kristin's death. I explained that relapses don't always occur when things are bad in a person's life. Sometimes, they happen when everything is going well and their future looks bright. The disease whispers that it wants to share in our good fortune. It could even be self-sabotage, a subliminal conviction that they don't deserve their happiness.

My struggle in coming to terms with my sister's death was maddening. I kept telling myself I could have saved her. *No, it's up to the addict to make that decision.* Yes, but I could have rescued her from herself. *It doesn't work that way, and you know it.* Why didn't she just come to me? *For the same reason, you didn't turn to anyone when you were in the thick of your addiction.* The bargaining stage of grief pushed its foot on my throat for the first years after her death.

I blamed those who sold her the drugs. I wanted them caught and punished to the fullest extent. No mercy. I wanted them to feel the pain they had caused. They were never found. Dealers don't leave business cards for a good time call. I blamed the drug itself. Fentanyl. It feeds on lives like some biblical plague humanity has unleashed upon itself. Just as it has done with countless others, it turned my sister into a statistic. The truth is, it was the fault of neither. My sister had invited them onto the stage. They played their roles perfectly. And as the curtain closed, they took their bow while Kristin was carried lifeless off to the wings.

My family has grown closer after Kristin passed away. In talking with them, I've learned so much about her—things

I wish I had known when she was alive. It saddens me to see how life's pressures, demands, and distractions can separate us from our loved ones. Often, we don't realize what's going on until it's too late.

If I could have one more day with Kristin, it would be someplace warm and green and quiet. There'd be nothing to distract us from each other. Our time would begin with an embrace, something I didn't do enough of when she was alive. I would hold her in my arms and feel her breathe again. After that, I'd ask questions just to get to know her better. Then I'd listen—something I think she needed in her life. What is your favorite movie? What is your favorite Christmas memory? When you were little, what did you want to be when you grew up? Tell me. What is your biggest fear? What is your deepest dream? What would you do if you won the lottery? Tell me. What is a secret you keep about yourself that you've never told anyone? What is the most embarrassing thing you've ever done? What is the happiest moment of your life? Tell me.

I want to know it all, and I want to hear it in her words, said with her laugh. As our day together draws to a close, it would end as it began, with an embrace. I've come to learn that there's absolutely nothing more valuable and more life-affirming than holding a loved one in my arms.

My sister's death has deepened my appreciation for family. I want to know everything about them and to let them know me just as well. When we get together, I do what I can to make it a memory for them to hold on to. I both teach and learn from them. I ask questions and truly listen. While I can't protect them from the harm of the world, they know I'm always here when they need me. The blink of an eye is a powerful span of time that can change everything we know and love.

These days, when I talk to a group about addiction, I don't just share my story—I share Kristin's as well. But not as a cautionary tale. I tell them what a beautiful person she was and the fatal choices she made for herself. As I speak, I hold up a picture of her so they can see her as a person. See her smile and the light in her eyes. I leave it to the listener to take away what touches them most. Hopefully, at least one person is changed. If so, then her life rises above her death.

I miss my sister every day. Sometimes, I smile at the thought of her. Other times, I cry. But always, there is a cloak of sadness I will never shed. One last thought: if I had one more day with my sister, I would tell her I love her. Something I didn't do enough when I had the chance.

Chapter Ten

The Love Between a Father and His Daughter

Tammy is married with two boys, and she writes about her beloved father, who was taken from this world at the young age of forty-seven due to cancer. Her father's name was Jim, and he bore an uncanny resemblance to Elvis. He even impersonated Elvis by singing some of his songs. Everyone who knew him called him Mr. J. He was a man who lived for his family and loved deeply. He had a passion for race cars and was an avid fan of the Bears, Cubs, and Hawks. He coached his children in baseball and bowling and had so much admiration for them.

Mr. J was a man who enjoyed making those around him laugh, whether he was telling jokes or playing pranks on them. You never knew what was coming your way! However, there was a serious side to him: the love he felt for his wife was remarkable! The pride he felt for his children was amazing, and there were times you could see the sparkle in his eyes when they were bowling.

Tammy stated, "I feel fortunate to have had one last conversation with my dad before he died. She stated that when she asked her dad if he was afraid to die, he told her he was not afraid but worried about leaving his family. There was so much more that he had left to do on this earth. My dad wanted to walk me down the aisle at my wedding and wanted to be there for his future grandchildren. He made me promise to help my mom find love again. This is something that I will forever regret because I never fulfilled his promise."

Tammy talked about what one more day with her dad would look like. They would be at their favorite place in the entire world, the bowling alley. Growing up, Tammy spent countless hours in the bowling alley with her parents and eventually became an amazing bowler herself. She is a soft-spoken woman who does not open up to many people, so it was an absolute honor to talk with her about her dad.

"What does my day look like?" Tammy pondered quietly for a moment. Then, she shared, "From the first second I saw him, I began to feel a sense of nervousness and uncertainty come over my entire body. Then, as he began to walk closer to me, I became excited. I had not felt this type of excitement in a very long time. I wrapped my arms around him and hugged him as hard as I could. I did not want to let go. I wanted to embrace this moment for the rest of my life! There was so much that I wanted to talk to him about. Where do I begin? I had dreamed about this day for twenty-five years, and now I sit here with my dad, completely overwhelmed with emotion."

Tammy began to talk about her day with me, stating that she discussed his childhood with him. She stated that she did not know much about her father's upbringing. She went on to talk about the conversation that they had about her dad's favorite family memories. "Oh, the beautiful memories we had as a family!" Tammy stated.

Tammy spent some of her day talking to her dad about her children and how proud he would be of each of them. She went on to tell her dad that her oldest son has his personality and that she feels his presence through both of her children.

Then, she began asking all of the questions that I believe we all want to know. She went on to talk about her fear of death. She described the anxiety and depression that set in when her dad was diagnosed with cancer and when he ultimately died.

Tammy stated, "Death of a loved one changes you forever. I thought that if I asked all of these questions, my anxiety would lessen. So, as depressing as this might sound, I asked my dad a lot of questions about death. For example, 'When you die, where do you go? Can you still communicate and see us? Are you spiritually around us every day? What do you feel like when you die? Are your loved ones who have died before you waiting for you? Are you given an explanation as to why you were chosen?"

When I asked her if her father had any answers to her questions, she simply said that her father smiled and told her that each afterlife experience is different and each person's experience is different. He assured her that those individuals who are spiritual seem to have more encounters with the deceased. He stated that when he died, he was at peace, and yes, his loved ones were waiting for him.

Lastly, Tammy's father said, "There is no rhyme or reason for why I was chosen to die so young, and it is not for you to continue the rest of your life questioning."

As their day came to an end, Tammy stated that she would apologize to her dad for never fulfilling her promise to help her mom find love again. She stated that, selfishly, she could not see her mom with another man. All these years later, she wished that her mom had found love again. In closing, Tammy stated, "Most of all, I loved being able to hug my dad and hear his laughter again. Oh, how I have missed his laugh!"

There is a saying that it is better to have loved and lost someone than to have never loved at all, and while that is true, the anguish that goes along with the loss is sometimes debilitating. Therefore, I chose to write about the topic of grief to give people hope in their lives and to allow them to never feel alone throughout their grieving process. It is up to each of us to write our own narrative; by allowing this, it is my hope that I will empower everyone who has contributed to this book.

Chapter Eleven

A Private Military Man

Michelle is a married woman with three beautiful daughters whom she adores. Her father, Lawrence, died when she was only seventeen years old. Describing him as a strong man who served his country in the Navy, she found his death to be unreal and difficult to comprehend. Lawrence suffered from the anguishing disease of alcoholism, which contributed to Michelle's confusion surrounding his death.

Alcoholism, a silent killer, was not openly discussed during Lawrence's lifetime. Similarly, the aftermath of the trauma that soldiers experienced overseas was rarely spoken about, and therapy was not sought after.

Michelle stated, "After my father's death, I was in complete denial. I waited for him to come home after work and have a brief conversation with me. But day after day, week after week, month after month, he never walked through the front door. It was at this point that I knew I was in complete denial about his death."

Lawrence was a reserved man who enjoyed assisting those around him. Kind-hearted and compassionate, he often aided the elderly, even going out of his way to drive them to doctor appointments. He volunteered at the church and was always willing to help fix anything that was broken. He was a gentle yet complicated man who truly loved his family.

He went out of his way for his children when he was able to, and he relished spending countless hours with them, playing baseball and softball. Even if he was tired of playing catch, he would catch with his other hand, all because he cherished his time with all three of his children. Michelle went on to say how much she missed his quirky sense of humor and his love for her.

Michelle expressed that if she could spend one day with her late father, she would choose to walk on the trails of Waterfall Glen. She stated, "Some of my best memories were of us walking the trails and talking with each other. I would like to speak with him about his upbringing. I did not know much about his childhood. I was young when he died, and I did not ask him a lot about himself. I regret not knowing more about my dad."

She added, "I knew my dad struggled with substance abuse, but we never spoke about it. I believe my mom did her best to protect me from some of the issues that my dad had with alcohol. In addition, I believe there was a lot my mom did not know about my dad. Like I mentioned before, my dad was a very private man who did not want to burden those around him."

Michelle stated that her day with her dad would be dedicated to getting to know him better or as much as he would share with her. She emphasized forgiveness and the significance of telling her dad that she forgave him for his struggles with alcoholism. She admitted that decades later, she realized that her father's illness was too powerful for him to combat.

Michelle shared, "After my dad's death, I found myself searching to understand him better. I yearned to know if he was proud of me or if he spoke highly of me to those he interacted with. My dad was a man of few words. He was quiet and did not express himself that well, but I knew he loved me in his own way. As I reflected on his death, I began questioning myself, *Why didn't I tell him how I really felt about him? Why didn't we spend more time together? Why does it take a death for people we haven't seen in years to come into town? Why do we take for granted the precious time we have on this earth with our loved ones?* I suppose it is because I thought I had more time with my dad. Ironically, after his death, I found a card from my dad, asking if we could go for a walk and catch up. Although this brought sadness to me, it also brought me comfort, knowing that my dad wanted to spend more time with me. I have learned throughout my life that I have to live for today and understand that there are no guarantees for tomorrow."

As Michelle's day came to an end, she would make her last turn on the trail with her father, and there would be her three beautiful daughters waiting for them. She stated that each of her daughters cautiously approached them. She introduced them to their grandfather and allowed each of them to have a conversation with their grandfather. By the end of the day, she would hope some of her questions about him would be answered and that she could finally let go of her guilt and come to accept her father's tragic death. Michelle expressed feelings of guilt for not saying more to him or helping him with his illness while he was alive. However, she has come to the realization that she could not help her dad; no one could.

Michelle stated, "I believe my dad is in a better place where he is happy and healthy and at peace with himself. In the end, that is all we ask for in this lifetime."

Chapter Twelve

A Family's Living Legacy

Many years ago, I met a dear friend who, for the first time in my life, clearly understood my story. I had never met anyone who could relate to me so much. It was uncanny to have such similar grief stories, but we did. We became very good friends, and no matter how much time passed in our lives, we could always pick up the phone and begin where we left off.

Jen is a beautiful human being whom I would describe as cautious in life: cautious with her career, cautious with her personal relationships, and cautious with her son, TJ. I admired her ability to approach life with such caution. Unlike her, I was not cautious; I was passionate about everything I did in my life—almost to a fault, I suppose.

After a decade of dating, Jen married Tom, the love of her life. They shared a love story that many people dreamed about their whole lives. I believe Jen sees a lot of similarities between Tom and her beloved father. Jen wrote one of the most beautiful letters about imagining one more day with her father.

Paul, Jen's father, was only forty-two years old when he suddenly passed away from a massive heart attack. Ironically, the doctor told the family that Paul was in the best shape of his life and could be Superman. That was not the case for

Paul; the autopsy showed that every artery was 100 percent blocked. There was a history of heart disease in the family, as Paul's twin brother died of a massive heart attack at thirty-four years old.

Paul was an outgoing and loving man who adored his large family. He loved hosting large family gatherings at his home. Paul's passion was cooking, and for a man who owned a family catering business in Chicago, you might expect him to want to relax on weekends. However, he found great joy in making meals for his family. When he was not busy running the business, he enjoyed golfing, landscaping, and playing softball with Jen. Jen remembered a lot of fond memories of her dad and herself. One of her earliest memories was waiting for her dad to get home. She would hug his leg tightly, and he would walk around with her hanging from it. She spoke about the daddy-daughter weekly date nights and how much they meant to her.

One of the greatest memories for the family was when they spent time at their cabin in northern Wisconsin. They spent quality time as a family in the great outdoors. Hiking, fishing, and spending time on the lake were all important to Paul. It was the quality time with his family that meant the most to him.

When I asked Jen to think about how she would spend one more day with her dad, she messaged me, stating that she needed time to think about the question. I never doubted for a second that she would not share her thoughts. I respected her cautious approach to her feelings, but deep down, I knew she would describe a poignant and beautiful day with her father.

Jen took some time to gather her thoughts and contemplate how she would spend a day with her departed father, if given the chance. However, when she finally did, it was a powerful story about the love between a father and his daughter.

Jen stated, "The moment I saw my father, I was ecstatic! I burst into tears and gave him the longest, tightest hug. I whispered to him, 'I love you, and I am so happy to see you.'"

Jen went on to say that she felt this overwhelming feeling throughout her body, and for the first time in a long time, she had a very difficult time controlling her emotions. After she contained her composure, she began talking about her wish to spend one more day with her father.

Jen described that they would be at the family cabin, enjoying the beautiful, warm sunset air. She expressed both joy and tears in her eyes as she envisioned them sitting together on the front porch, just like they used to. They would be listening to the loons, eagles, deer, and birds while enjoying each other's conversation.

Jen stated, "There is no greater gift than sharing in all of God's creation. My father and I relished the times when we sat peacefully on the front porch and watched in amazement at what God had created."

One of Jen's greatest joys in life is TJ, her adorable son. She stated that she would seek advice from her dad on parenting and everything else that goes along with it. She would reminisce about childhood and her faith. She would ask all the questions that all of us think about when a loved one dies without seeing our accomplishments: "Are you proud of me? Am I a good mom? Am I doing things right in life? What more should I accomplish in my life?"

Jen and I could talk for hours about the questions she had for her father, as I had the same ones. Since our dads died really young, it's natural to wonder if they are proud of us and if we're being the best moms to our children. We even joked about whether we were ever doing things right in our lives—after all, are we ever doing things necessarily right? When it comes to life accomplishments, I told her I believe the greatest achievement is building our family! Nothing else compares to creating a supportive and loving family!

Jen continued to recount her day with her dad. She introduced him to her family, and they spent one last evening enjoying a bonfire and dinner, watching the joy in TJ's eyes as he talked with his Grandpa Paul. As the night drew to a close, Jen started to feel anxious and empty, knowing that she had to say goodbye. She hugged her dad tightly once more and thanked him for being an amazing father and for spending the day with her family, especially her son.

Remember grief is a journey into the unknown. However, always remember that you are not alone. There is always someone else going through their own journey. Each person's journey might look different, but I have often found solace in sharing my journey with a perfect stranger—someone who would listen to me without judgment.

Perfect strangers were the ones who brought me the most hope in my life. Just having someone who let me talk about my grief and the devastation that my father's death caused on my life was all I needed. And you know what? I learned that those perfect strangers were also dealing with their own grief and had their own stories to tell. That is why these courageous conversations were so meaningful to me.

Chapter Thirteen

The Story of Two Brothers

This is the story of Rich. He is a husband, a father, and a grandfather. He has dedicated his entire life to supporting not only his immediate family but also his extended family. Rich is an unselfish man who has faced more than his share of grief in life. However, he picked up the pieces of his life and took care of those around him. Rich is a proud Italian man who does for others without asking for anything in return. When I began writing this book, his family was one of the first to whom I reached out.

Rich has endured a lot of grief, but he expressed his heartfelt wish to spend one last day with his beloved brother, Frank.

Frank was thirty-four years old when he passed away from lymphoma. He was a husband, an uncle, and the father of two children. Frank was a wonderful father to his young children and a dedicated husband. Frank and Rich had a very close relationship and often spent a lot of time together, along with their families.

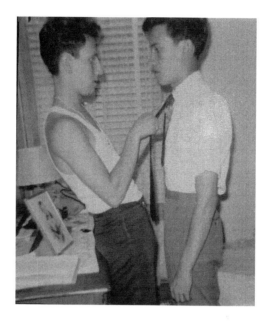

Rich envisioned spending one more day with Frank. In his mind's eye, the moment he saw his younger brother, joy overwhelmed him. They hugged each other tightly, and for that one moment in time, they were back to where they were when they were kids. With much emotion in Rich's heart, he told Frank how much he missed him. Together, they reminisced about the specially made Italian clothing that they would both purchase. Rich laughed and said that Frank always knew when he was borrowing his shirts. They talked about the good times they had with friends at the pool hall where they used to hang out.

Rich described the most important conversation they had on that day: family. Family was very important to both of them; it was sacred. They talked for hours about their families, with Rich sharing updates on everyone's lives and accomplishments. Rich assured Frank that he would always be there for each of Frank's children, dedicating countless hours to advising and supporting them as they grew up. Over the years, the family remained extremely close, with Rich steadfastly by their side every step of the way.

As the day came to an end, Rich embraced Frank one last time and told him how grateful he was for having this one special moment in life to see him again. Rich promised his younger brother that he would continue to watch over his children and grandchildren, vowing to make him proud!

Chapter Fourteen

Remembering Anna

As the years go by, grief remains. It might look different, but you never forget the death of a loved one. This is the story of Kathy. She is a wife, a mother, and a grandmother to one grandchild. Her life revolves around her family. When asked whom she would spend her day with, Kathy didn't hesitate: her mother, Anna. Kathy expressed how overjoyed she would be to see her mother again.

When asked about her mother, Kathy's face lit up. She eloquently described Anna as a beautiful and kind-hearted soul, emphasizing her compassion and love. Despite battling cancer for much of her life, Anna prioritized caring for her five children. Kathy noted that anyone who knew her loved her.

Kathy began to imagine one more day with her mom, and during their time together, they were in their old house reminiscing about family. Kathy talked about Anna's grandchildren, Matt and Kurt, expressing pride in all of their accomplishments in life. Kathy stated that both of them turned out to be compassionate, kind, loving, and generous young men. As for her grandson Kyle, he is Kathy's pride and joy. Kathy stated this about Kyle: "There is not a day that goes by that I don't feel blessed to have this little guy in my life. He has a beautiful heart and a smile that lights up the universe. He is a creative boy who brings so much joy to my life!"

Kathy and I have had many conversations over the years about the emptiness that grief brings into our lives and how difficult some days can be for us. So, when grief sneaks up on you when you least expect it, take a breath and do the best you can do to ride the wave.

Chapter Fifteen

For the Love of Brian

When I began writing this book, I knew there would be wonderful stories that would be told, but what I did not realize was the number of people who had loved ones who died so young. It made me think about the fact that there are no guarantees for tomorrow.

Kevin's story about his identical twin, Brian, deeply resonated with me. Perhaps it was because Brian was a young man who died at the age of thirty-nine from Lou Gehrig's disease. Maybe it was because every time I talked to Kevin, I could see the pain in his eyes—something I knew all too well.

Kevin's entire world changed when Brian died. He stated that after his twin passed away, he did a lot of soul-searching, questioning the meaning and direction of his life. Eventually, he made the bold decision to leave his position in the business world and pursue a degree in theology to explore these questions further. I admire Kevin's courage in making a leap of faith and changing career paths. From my own observations, Kevin has a knack for uncovering the deeper meaning in life and serves those on a similar quest through his ministries. His deep religious faith has been a guiding force for him since Brian's death.

On the last day of their vacation in Hawaii, Kevin and his wife visited a secluded beach. Kevin let his wife know that he was not going to go in the water because they had to go home shortly, and he didn't want to have to shower again. They sat watching the impressive waves and the people boogie-boarding in the surf. Amid that scene, Kevin heard a voice in his head, "Come on, look at those waves! This is your last day. You can't pass them up!"

"With a sense of thrill and relief, I knew it was Brian talking to me," Kevin recounted. "It had been thirty-one years since Brian and I were in Hawaii bodysurfing together. We were so close as twins. We could finish each other's sentences and had a deep bond on many levels. While other family members have felt Brian's presence since his passing, I never did, despite our strong bond. It puzzled me until today.

"Brian was with me on that secluded beach, telling me to get up and ride the waves. I began to imagine spending one more day with him. We reminisced about our time in Maui, laughing about how Brian would ride the waves before getting slammed to the beach floor, injuring his shoulder. That put an end to our golf rounds, tennis games, and other physical contests; we were both highly competitive.

"After spending some time in the ocean, we walked up to a higher point on the beach and settled on the smoothest rock we could find. We talked about our lives, our family, and friends, delving into the impact of Brian's disease on his body. We spoke of our time in the outer banks of North Carolina one year after Brian's diagnosis. We reminisced about bodysurfing and Brian masterfully riding the waves, extracting every bit of enjoyment from them. However, I noticed that he remained lying face-down in the shallow, receding water, unable to get up. It was at this point that I ran to grab him. Thinking it would be difficult to get him up, I braced myself for his weight, but to my surprise, he was much lighter than I anticipated. Brian had lost much of his muscle mass. I think it hit both of us at that moment that the disease was progressing rapidly. For Brian, he knew all the activities he loved to do would soon become impossible. Unfortunately, two months after that North Carolina trip, Brian took his last breath."

With a glint in his eye and that sly grin of his, Brian challenged, "Kevin, don't be a scaredy-cat. Take on those waves!"

Kevin recalled, "I got up, took off my sunglasses, and told my wife that I was going in! Remembering Brian's body-surfing incident, I took note of the submerged rock that I had banged my shin on and made my way out to the breakers. I could feel Brian's eyes light up as I climbed out of the surf. I could hear Brian yelling, 'Don't you love letting go, being lifted and carried, feeling the power of the ocean and the effervescence of the surf that leaves you wanting to keep going?' As I caught my breath and cleared the salty water from my nose, I nodded in agreement with him."

Kevin sighed before continuing, expressing, "With our day coming to a close, I felt a sense of somberness. As we walked far above the ocean to our rock, there was some silence between us, almost as if both of us were contemplating what we wanted to say to each other before the day ended. With a rare expression of seriousness, Brian urged me to live my life to the fullest. I will never forget his last words to me. Brian said, 'Don't forget that riding a wave is all about letting go of life for that one moment in time and trusting in the power of God to lift you up and carry you through life's tribulations and giving you the will and strength to keep going on. I feel like the luckiest guy in the world, Kevin!'"

Kevin gave Brian a huge hug and thanked him for a wonderful and memorable day that would remain etched in his memory for a lifetime.

Kevin has hung onto his conversation with Brian since his death twenty-five years ago. He shared with me that his brother was a man of his word and lived his life fully and joyfully. Kevin knows that his brother is close by, watching over all of them from the other side of the veil, experiencing a new kind of life, just as he did when he preceded him into this life as a beloved older brother . . . by three minutes.

I remember reading and then re-reading Kevin's wish to have one more day with Brian. I couldn't help but imagine their day and the power of the love that these two brothers shared. Some may say that it was love that was cut way too short, but Kevin doesn't look at it that way. Instead, it's a love that continues to inspire Kevin to live a little differently, love a little harder, and remember his beloved brother through his active faith. One could say that Kevin is Brian's living legacy, carrying on where he left off in this life.

Chapter Sixteen

Barb the Soft-Spoken Warrior

To know Barb was to love her—a soft-spoken woman who would much rather listen to those around her and relish their stories than to be the life of the party. I believe this is what I loved most about Barb. She was one of the kindest human beings that I would be blessed to have ever known.

Our families were connected by our parents' decades of friendship. Our parents were the best of friends. Barb was a mother, wife, grandmother, and friend to all who knew her. Barb was a warrior, a woman who fought cancer courageously, a woman who never showed her family her fears but rather protected all of them.

When I asked her youngest child, Kristen, if she would write about spending one more day with her mom, she became emotional but poured her heart into it. Kristen expressed that she would spend the day at her mom's house, reminiscing on the couch like they used to.

Kristen imagined talking to her mom about the crazy times of COVID, stocking up on toilet paper, bleach, and groceries, and adapting to the new age of socializing with everyone through Zoom. She shared with her mom how she would have been crocheting a lot of masks, although they would not meet safety standards. The two of them laughed about the crazy times going on in the world.

Throughout the day, they talked about so much, including how Mike, Kristen's dad, had lost a hearing aid because of the mask he was wearing. He was in the parking lot for hours looking for it until he realized that the hearing aid had fallen into his shirt.

***

To see my mom laugh and light up as I told her the stories was the greatest joy in my life. I always loved her laugh and the glow that came upon her face when we spoke about family and life.

During the day, my mom got up from the couch and brought an album of photos to share with me. We spent hours talking about all the wonderful pictures in the album. My mom had the greatest memory and shared many stories with me.

To see my mom travel down memory lane was an absolute inspiration to me, a moment I will never forget. After we finished looking at photos of our loved ones, my mom brought out her jewelry box. She began talking about every single piece of jewelry and the meaning behind each piece. One piece in particular was a charm bracelet that held a special place in her heart. As she spoke about each charm, it was almost like she had gone back in time, reliving the memories and importance of each one.

What I loved most about my mom was how positive she was about life, even when battling for her own life. She had such strength and a pleasant disposition. My mom found meaning out of everything in her life. One thing that brought her immense joy was her beloved Millie doll, which she cherished and cared for deeply. Now I have the doll and continue to care for it in her memory. Every time I look at Millie, I think of my mom. I won't lie—there are times in my life when I mourn the loss of my mom. However, I know that she lives on in all of us, and I know that I have to keep going on in my life in order to carry on where she left off.

Chapter Seventeen

Remembering Riley

G rieving the death of a child is an inexplicable, heart-wrenching, and overwhelming experience, and few understand this better than Cindy. When I began the journey of writing a book on grief and the desire for one more day with a loved one, Cindy messaged me and stated that she would be interested in contributing to the book. It wasn't until I began reading her story that I truly grasped the depth of her experience. Her journey through grief was absolutely raw and inspirational.

Throughout Cindy's pregnancy, she faced high-risk situations that led to visits to the emergency room in attempts to prevent early delivery. Unfortunately, Cindy's son Riley was born at twenty-two and a half weeks and survived for only fifty-two minutes before passing away. The insurmountable feelings of disbelief and shock took over Cindy's world entirely. She stated, "How could something so bad happen to my first-born son, my husband, and me? How could an innocent baby be taken away from me?" Cindy shared the deep love she felt while holding Riley and cherishing the brief time she had with him, but at the same time, she struggled with the unfairness of life.

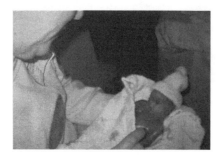

"Riley's loss left an emptiness that I didn't realize was so problematic in my life until many years later, possibly because I was in survival mode," said Cindy. After the death of a loved one, it is human nature to go into survival mode. The brain tells the mind to keep going, but sometimes, we bury our emotions deep down along the way. When you're a parent, you never imagine having to bury a child. It is human nature to think that our children will lay us to rest. Such sorrow and pain never go away, but in time, you find ways to cope with insurmountable grief.

Cindy reminisced about what her day would look like with Riley. She began by stating that she would take a closer look at his body and facial features. "I only had fifty-two minutes with him, and I was so overwhelmed with emotion that I did not study his features. I only remembered his perfect button nose, the same nose that my daughter Gabby would have almost three years to the date of Riley's death. Gabby was our miracle baby. She was born with multiple medical issues, but I truly believe Riley was her guardian angel," Cindy said.

"Riley and I would sit on a blanket under a tree near the front of our house, or if he wanted to, we would lie on the hammock, like his sister and I always did. I would take the time to take a million pictures of us together. I would talk with Riley about his sister, Gabby, who fought so hard to be brought into this world. I would tell Riley that after many years of grieving and asking why he died, I would finally understand the reason. Riley sacrificed his life for Gabby's life. He was her guardian angel, who was able to get her through all of her health issues. He watched out for her and made certain that she survived. As I talked to Riley, I noticed this little smile on his face and a sparkle in his eye, almost like he was telling me that I was right," explained Cindy.

Cindy wanted her day with her son to be extraordinary, so she invited Gabby to spend some time with him. She wanted to watch her two beautiful children together before inviting other family members to their day. "I would relish having one day with Gabby and Riley, listening to them talk about sibling stuff and running around playing with one another. I could see Gabby showing Riley around everywhere and playing hide and seek. I am most happy listening to them whisper and giggle at each other. I am in awe seeing the similarities in their overall being. I would want Riley to know that his sister is smart, intelligent, and strong because of his own sacrifice. Later on in the day, my family would come to see Riley. He would be embraced with so much love and laughter by all. As the day came to a close, I would be sad but thankful that Gabby was able to meet her brother. I would tell both of my children that they might not physically be together in this world, but they will be forever connected. As I held both of them close to my body, I whispered to Riley, 'You will be forever remembered because your legacy will live on in all of your family. I love you, my beautiful boy,'" Cindy exclaimed.

Chapter Eighteen

To Know Paul Was to Love Him

I remember growing up in the same neighborhood as Paul. For years, we attended the same small school district in a rural town where everyone knew each other. Paul and I hung out with different people throughout the years, but I remember him fondly. He was the type of friend that everyone wanted in their lives. He never had a mean word to say about anyone. He was always joking around and lived to make people happy. I will always remember Paul for his larger-than-life personality and his heart of gold!

Paul came from a large family and was the sixth of seven children. Alina, Paul's older sister, wrote about her wish to spend one last day with her younger brother. She described Paul as funny, athletic, and witty. She stated that her brother was the life of the party, and he always wanted everyone around him to have a great time. However, Paul had a vulnerable side. Alina saw the pain that existed within him when falling in and out of love with someone, and she saw the sadness in him when talking about family relationships.

Paul had a heart of gold and was deeply hurt when relationships were broken. Alina stated, "Paul was more than a brother to me. He was my dancing partner, handyman, babysitter, coworker, and best friend. We had a connection in life that no one could take away. For my children, he was their coach, best friend, and uncle who adored them. Paul was a proud uncle who took great care of his three nephews. My boys adored Uncle Paul!"

Paul lived passionately, loved deeply, and cared deeply for his family. However, Paul struggled with life stressors. When Paul showed up at her house unannounced, Alina knew that something was bothering him. They would spend countless hours on the back deck, talking about life, work, family, and stress. Paul's greatest gift was passionately loving those around him, but it was also his greatest pitfall. For Paul, it was easier to worry about those around him and try to take care of them rather than help himself. He was a selfless human being who had his own struggles in life.

On December 22, 2018, Alina went to check on Paul, only to find the police at his apartment building.

***

I will never forget that day for as long as I live. A police officer came up to me and said he was very sorry, informing me that Paul was gone. I dropped to my knees and screamed, and my scream to this day still rings in my ears. I found myself at the foot of Paul's car, just steps away from where I had dropped him off two days earlier. I was at a loss, unsure of whom to call or what to say to my mom. I sat frozen in a state of shock, asking myself why he did not call me or come over. He always reached out when he was feeling depressed. But this time was different. Days later, it became clear: Paul could not cope with the pain any longer.

Paul died two days before Christmas by suicide. I have gone through that day a million times in my head, wondering why. Why, why, why did he die? In the terror of reality, I knew he was no longer hurting. God had finally given him the peace he needed. I see him in my dreams. When I am sitting on my deck, I feel his presence. I visit him frequently at the cemetery, and I hear his voice. Two days after Paul died, I heard his voice telling me he was sorry, but he was all right. Deep down, I knew he was all right because, for the first time in his life, he was at peace.

Paul struggled with many inadequacies that persisted throughout his lifetime. Growing up in a large family meant he did not receive much individual attention. Though our family did its best, we were not perfect, and I believe this had a lasting impact on Paul.

Paul was an amazing man who struggled deeply in his personal life. He masked his insecurities by drinking. Drinking was his way of coping with depression and anxiety. Losses in his life impacted him greatly. Although Paul loved deeply, he often sabotaged relationships. His unresolved childhood issues and difficulty processing emotions surfaced in his adult life, hindering his ability to maintain successful relationships. In addition, he had a difficult time settling down and planning for the future, which also affected relationships, especially as he approached his forty-fifth birthday. If I could have one wish, it would be to have one more day with Paul.

On our special day together, this was how I imagined it: I was sitting in my backyard on the deck, watching the sun settling in the distance, and from afar, I saw Paul's shadow walking toward me. Tears welled up in my eyes as I approached him. I hugged him and told him how much I loved him. I took in his scent and his overall being, then told him how much I missed him. With a huge grin on his face, he hugged me and told me not to cry and that he loved me dearly.

I told him how I slept with his jacket near me for weeks after his death just so I could smell his scent. I felt closest to him when I wore his jacket. It has been over two years since his death, but I still hold onto his jacket.

Then, I offered him a beer and put on Toad the Wet Sprocket, his favorite band. He asked me how I had been since his death. I put on a brave face and told him, "I'm struggling but standing strong." Paul accepted my answer with confidence because he admired my strength. This was an area in which he struggled within his own life.

Paul offered me advice on raising my boys because he loved them so much, treating them as if they were his own children despite not being a father himself.

We enjoyed a nice dinner together and talked about music. Paul loved music. He often suggested songs for me to sing. He loved listening to me sing. Ironically, he also offered me relationship advice as his way of giving back to me.

I knew our time was nearing when Paul began to get restless. As much as I did not want him to leave, I knew I had to let go. We hugged longer than usual because we both knew our time was coming to an end. I told him, "I will always love you," and with a crackle in his voice, he told me, "I will love you forever."

He looked me in the eyes and told me that he would be fine and that I did everything I could to help him. I began to cry as he said, "Love you, sis." As he turned away from me, he said, "See ya later."

I saw the shadow of his body leaving the yard. As I looked up to the sky, I saw the sun shining from beneath the clouds, and at that point in time, I knew my baby brother was going to be all right. This day gave me such gratitude for the time we had together. I finally felt a sense of peace in my life. This day is a memory I'll remember for the rest of my life.

I consider myself lucky. I came to know all sides of my brother and found peace and understanding of his choice in the final moments of his life. I'm blessed to love and accept Paul for who he was. I'm grateful to know that he watches over my family.

Chapter Nineteen

A Beautiful Life Gone Too Soon

This is the story of Kathy, a mother of three children, a grandmother to eleven, and a widow at the age of forty-three. An outsider looking into Kathy's life could say that she was the matriarch of her entire family—a strong and proud woman who vowed never to marry again after the sudden death of her husband, Bob.

Kathy's story began at the early age of fifteen when she met Bob. They were high school sweethearts and the loves of each other's lives. They had a fairytale life and were married at nineteen and twenty. Their plan was to marry soon after graduating from high school and to have children young so they could be young enough to relish in all of their children's activities. Unfortunately, life doesn't always go according to plan.

Bob and Kathy were married for twenty-three years before his sudden death. At the young age of forty-four, Bob died of a sudden heart attack, leaving behind three children and Kathy. Life, as Kathy had once known it, would be forever changed. She did her best to move on, but the sudden devastation took a toll on everyone. Kathy was left to pick up the pieces. Bob had been the sole financial provider for the family. Although Kathy worked, his death brought drastic financial changes. However, even in death, Bob had planned to take care of his family financially.

Kathy described how her day with Bob would unfold if she were granted one more day with him.

***

I would want to know why he missed all of the warning signs of a heart attack. Why didn't he talk to me and tell me he wasn't feeling well? Why didn't he let me help him? There were so many signs that I learned about after his death. Soon after Bob's death, the family lost their beloved dog, who was tragically hit by a car. I wondered if Bob wanted the dog in heaven with him because of his connection with him.

I feel that having one more day with Bob would allow me to talk about everything that he missed over the past two decades. Our conversation would be about the beautiful family that we created together and the success of each of our children.

I would begin our conversation by sarcastically letting him know how much I appreciated walking our daughter down the aisle at her wedding. Next to losing him, walking my daughter down the aisle was the second most difficult event of my life. I would tell him how absolutely stunning she looked on her wedding day and how much she reminded me of him!

I would tell Bob, "She married a good man who had that same look in his eyes as you did when I married you. Our daughter was not only beautiful, but she was strong on her wedding day."

Besides talking about our children, I would talk to Bob about his eleven grandchildren and how special each of them is to me. They have all grown up to be amazing human beings, and I know that he would cherish each one of them.

During our day together, I would first take Bob to see his eldest son, also named Bob, at his doctor's office. I would listen to them catch up with each other and just appreciate the time they had together. Then, we would travel to Chicago to visit his second son, Nick, who is a sergeant in the Chicago Police Department. Lastly, I would take him to see his youngest and only daughter, Becky. Once again, I would relish watching them catch up with each other. Becky and her father have always shared a special relationship, one filled with unique and mutual love.

As our day comes to an end, I would tell Bob that not a day has passed without thoughts of him. We had a true love that many dream about in a lifetime—a love that I would never find with anyone else. Although our time in life was cut short, I am blessed to have had twenty-three amazing years with him. Even though Bob was not present for all the monumental milestones of his children and grandchildren, I have to believe that he is watching from afar and smiling down from above.

Chapter Twenty

A Genuine Darling
On and Off the Ice

There are those people in your life that you meet once, but they leave an indelible mark on your life. For my family, that person was Scott Darling, an NHL hockey player for the Blackhawks and Carolina Hurricanes. I can personally tell you that it was not Scott's fame as a Blackhawk that left a mark on me. Rather, it was his huge heart and the way he talked to my young son when he signed his jersey. His soft-spoken disposition and kind heart left a lasting impression on all of us who met him.

I'm sure you are reading this asking how I know Scott Darling. Scott's mom, Cindy, is a dear friend of mine and someone I am fortunate to have in my life. She is the person I can confide in about anything in my life. One of her best qualities is her ability to sit quietly and listen without judgment. I remember all the heart-to-heart conversations we have had at work. In addition, I knew even on my most difficult day, I could walk into her office, close the door, and decompress. I always told Cindy that someday I aspire to be like her—a kind-hearted soul who would do anything for you. By the way, she gives the best hugs!

Fast forward to May of 2019, I will never forget the phone call from Cindy when she told me about the tragic death of her ex-husband and Scott's dad. It was devastating listening to her talk about how much she was worried about her three children. Cindy discussed the tragic drowning of her ex-husband and its impact on all of them. I remember stopping her and asking how she was doing. She simply said, "I am all right. I don't know what to do for any of my kids."

I shared some advice with her about the grieving process and said all she could do was be there for her kids and just listen. I knew Cindy could support her kids because she was a very strong human being.

Over the years, Cindy and I would talk about family, life, and work. She was the type of person who always seemed genuinely interested in whatever I had to say, even if I was just rambling. One day, while we were out to lunch, I brought up the grief book I was working on. I began reading some chapters to her and shared how cathartic writing the book had been for me. My main goal, I explained, was to help others who were going through their own grieving process.

Cindy shared Scott's journey after his dad died. She told me that Scott had become a comedian, using humor to process life's challenges. I was absolutely in awe of what she was saying because incorporating comedy into this book was a goal of mine.

Reflecting on individuals with special talents, such as comedians, actors, singers, artists, and musicians, I realized they all have something in common: they use their talents both for entertaining others and as a form of self-therapy. This insight underscores why artists are so talented—they are emotionally driven by forces bigger than themselves. Cindy and I understand this emotional drive intimately, having raised talented young adults ourselves.

I have always been mindful of maintaining boundaries in my friendship with Cindy, and I never wanted to blur the lines. However, on this particular day, I felt compelled to ask her if Scott would be interested in contributing to the book. So, here we are. I'm humbled and absolutely honored to share Scott's story of how he handled his own grieving process.

Let me tell you, Scott is an absolute inspiration on so many levels. He has taught me how being a comedian helped him in coping with adversity. Scott Darling is an authentic, humble, and vulnerable human being who is keen to understand those who may seem quiet or shy or even appear uncomfortable. He goes out of his way to put them at ease by striking up conversations.

During my interview with Scott, he said, "Ever since I was a child, I would observe the room that I was in and find the person who appeared uncomfortable, and I would begin a conversation. I wanted the person to simply be happy. I know deep down in my soul how it feels to not always be happy.

So, I have learned through my own therapeutic journey and comedy to turn my pain and hardships into humor!"

I remember my first phone conversation with Scott. I missed his call because I was in the middle of getting an MRI. (Yes, that's what I was busy doing. Fun times!) Shortly after the MRI, I texted him back that I would call him in five minutes. I called Scott, but he did not pick up, so I tried again.

Eventually, I heard on the other end of the phone, "Hello," after a long pause.

I said, "Hi, Scott. This is Becky."

There was another pause, and then Scott remarked, "Oh, it says Michael Caruso."

With a touch of humor, I responded, "Yes, that's my husband. He pays the phone bill."

Later, as I reflected on our conversation, it dawned on me that Scott must be cautious with the people he surrounds himself with in his life. He has to put a wall up around himself to shield against those who might have ulterior motives—a reality many of us take for granted.

Honestly, I found this aspect of Scott's character truly admirable, and it strongly reminded me of his mom. Their similarities are uncanny. Both of them are humble, kind, and patient individuals who can open up and be vulnerable with those they trust. Please don't mistake any of these characteristics as weaknesses. On the contrary, both of them are keen on who they allow into their circle of friends, only placing their full trust in those they hold dear.

Going through the grieving process has a way of manipulating our thoughts and feelings. It can create a deep-seated fear of trusting anyone with our deepest feelings, lest we be misunderstood or rejected. Therefore, for some people, the process of grief can be lonely.

As I began to talk more to Scott, I learned that he also had his own story to tell about grief, and when we spoke, I have to admit it was really emotional. See, we all have these perceived notions of one another, and let's face it, we stereotype each other.

When you look at Scott, you see this six-foot-six-inch larger-than-life athlete who has more success than many of us can dream about in a lifetime. However, what we don't see is the vulnerable man that Scott has become due to the tragedy that he has suffered in his life. Scott is no different than the average human being. He has emotions and feelings just like everyone else.

When Scott learned about the book I was writing, he immediately agreed to contribute at his mom's request. I have to admit—I was not prepared for our first phone conversation. It was filled with honesty, transparency, and a lot of emotion. We began to talk about Scott's dad's tragic and untimely death, and as he spoke, I could hear the pain in his voice. It is an agonizing pain that only someone who has lived through grief can remotely understand. I say this because everyone's journey through grief is different.

Scott began to courageously talk about finding out about his father's death.

***

The Memphis State Police Department called me and asked if they had the correct number for Scott Darling. I replied yes. I knew immediately that something terrible had happened to my father. The phone call was the worst call I have ever received in my life. I don't even think I could use the words to describe my feelings. They began to tell me that they were only able to identify my father by the tattoo on his forearm, which depicted me. They explained that he had drowned.

Immediately after I hung up the phone, I threw up all over my kitchen floor. The immense pain and suffering that I felt were indescribable, and knowing that I had to tell my family made the situation even more unbearable.

For the past four years since my father's death, I have yearned for one more day with him. My relationship with my father was complicated for most of my life, and for a long time, we did not talk. There was a lot that I didn't know about my father, and at times, he seemed like a perfect stranger to me. There has not been a day that has gone by that I haven't thought about what I would say to my dad. So, during our day together, I would ask him about the happiest memory of his life and how it made him feel.

My father was not a man who talked about emotions or feelings, so I would hope that we could take the time to talk about him and his childhood. I'd like to know if there was one thing he could change about his life, what would it be? I think his answer would tell a lot about his character and how he viewed himself. In turn, I would want to know what he felt was the biggest mistake he made in his life. While we have all made mistakes, I would wonder whether we would agree on some of the ones he had made while alive.

There has not been a day that has gone by that I have not thought about my father's untimely death. I wonder about what his last words would have been to me. I wonder every day if I made him proud of the human being I turned into. I would take the time during my day to get to know my father on a deeper level. I would express to him how he made me feel throughout my childhood and even into my young adulthood. Whether he liked what I said or not, I would find the courage deep within me to speak my truth.

After our conversation, I would bring my father back to the Houston Aeros Arena, where we used to spend time together watching hockey games. However, this time, I would do everything differently. As we walked into the empty arena, I would make sure not to move away from him when he sat next to me. I remember the look on his face that day when I got up and moved away from him. He was disappointed and asked me why I did not want to sit next to him. What my father did not realize was that I struggled to sit next to anyone. I didn't feel comfortable with physical proximity due to the trauma I had faced in my life. However, I could not bring myself to explain this to him. If I could do it all over again, I would shower him with hugs and express to him that although our relationship was complicated, I still loved and forgave him.

***

Scott and I spoke extensively about adversity in our lives and how it made us stronger and wiser human beings. Scott remarked, "I have had a lot of baggage in my life that could have destroyed me or made me stronger. I decided to take my baggage and channel it through being an NHL Hockey Player and a comedian. When I perform on stage, it is an escape for me. It allows me to emotionally forget about my own issues."

He also shared about Ian Bagg, a Canadian comedian who would end his show by saying, "I hope I helped you escape the world for 90 minutes." This saying has always resonated with me because comedy is my therapeutic escape. When I see the smiles and laughter on people's faces, it brings me happiness.

For someone who deals with anxiety and depression on a daily basis, it takes a lot of preparation to perform on stage. However, it is worth all the preparation in the world to use dark humor to make people laugh.

I will never forget the quote Robin Williams stated: "I think the saddest people always try their hardest to make people happy because they know what it is like to feel absolutely worthless, and they don't want anyone to feel like that."

In essence, comedians face their own personal struggles just like everyone else. We simply choose to channel them through comedy. Throughout my grieving process, I have used both therapy and comedy as a means to cope with my journey.

I believe each person has their own different ways of grieving. Personally, I continue to grieve about my father's untimely death, and I'm also affected by my mother's previous battles with breast cancer. She is the pillar of strength for our family, and I constantly worry about her health. Just because she is in remission doesn't erase the worry and fear I feel.

Throughout my own personal struggles, my mother weathered every storm with me, and for that, I will forever love her. To this day, she is my number-one fan and comes to my shows. Even when I tell jokes about her, I can hear her laugh the loudest. The moral of my story is just like you, I am human, and I grieve deeply. However, it is important to find a therapeutic strategy that is right for you.

Chapter Twenty-One

Fear of the Unknown

E ven as an adolescent, I thrived from structure in my life. I needed constant routines in place. Without routine, I felt a sense of uncertainty in my life. So, you could only imagine what a sudden death in my family would do to me. My dad's death changed everything in my life, including my outlook on life itself.

Every day, I waited for him to come home or to be present at a softball game. I waited for him to sit down at dinner and ask me about my day. I waited for him to spend time with me. All of that changed in the blink of an eye. Even after he died, I still waited for him, especially during all my softball games.

The life I had once known was gone, and the structure I relied on had vanished. Therefore, I needed to find a new normal. Trying to find a new normal seems like an unbearable task after the death of a loved one, especially when you are an adolescent.

The adolescent years bring with them a sense of entitlement, egocentrism, and many grandiose behaviors. These years bring a sense of invincibility! There is no fear that an adolescent faces during these years, or so one would think. I would love to admit that I was invincible and that the sky was the limit, but honestly, after my dad's death, I had a debilitating fear of the unknown. I had always looked to my dad for reassurance in life. He was there to encourage me every step of the way. Now that he was gone, what did my future hold? As an adolescent who once had direction and purpose, I feared what was to come next in my life.

There was no roadmap to guide me throughout my journey of fear. I remember searching for the definition of "fear," hoping for some guidance on my emotions and whether they were normal. I tried to intellectualize my feelings. Maybe it was an escape from the deep and agonizing pain within me.

I learned that fear is an unpleasant emotion that causes both emotional and physical pain. The emotional pain after the death of a loved one is incomprehensible. There are not enough words to capture the pain that one feels, but most importantly, it is normal to fear your own livelihood. When someone dies, it is only natural to fear death. As for the physical aspect of what fear does to the body, each person's experience looks different. Constant fear took over my life. Was I going to die next from illness? Was my body functioning properly? Was I going to die from a heart attack like my dad? The constant battle of dealing with fear is a reality for all of us, but how we conquer our fear is another story.

So, what did I do to combat my feelings? I began reading self-help books to help me overcome this sense of fear I felt in my life. I learned a lot about myself throughout the years. I learned that my feelings of fear and despair were real; however, my thoughts, as real as they might have been, were distorted.

For example, for several months, I refused to go out with my friends. One might ask why I felt this way. Well, I thought if I left my mom and went out, something terrible might happen to her, and she might die. For years, I would not leave the house on Friday the 13th. Why? Because on Friday, November 13, my father suddenly died. Therefore, in my mind, if I stayed home on that date, I wouldn't be at risk of losing my own life. Superstitious? Yes. My reality? Yes!

After my father's death, I had a difficult time sleeping. I had a constant fear that my mom was going to die in her sleep. Therefore, I would check on her throughout the night to make certain that she was breathing. All these feelings were real, but I knew that I needed to do something to help myself because I was emotionally and physically exhausted. I could not keep living in fear! Fear had taken over my entire life, and at times, it was debilitating.

I learned many years later about cognitive behavioral therapy (CBT) and the positive impact that it could have on a person who lived in fear and suffered from anxiety and depression. For me, I had nothing to lose; it was worth learning more about this therapeutic approach. CBT seriously gave me a new perspective on life.

CBT is used with people who have a variety of psychological problems, such as anxiety and depression. CBT helped me to understand my feelings. As I mentioned before, my feelings were real, but they were distorting my entire physiological being. The fear I felt began to make me anxious in my life. So, not only was I dealing with fear, but I was also anxious all the time.

Anxiousness can create all kinds of cognitive distortions that impact the way we live. What are cognitive distortions? Simply put, they are exaggerated and/or irrational thoughts that a person thinks about all the time. They are thoughts that distort the way human beings feel about themselves. Therefore, a person is not able to see life through a clear lens. The use of CBT assists an individual to recognize their distorted thoughts and begin to slowly deal with each thought in order to live a more peaceful life.

Once I was able to recognize how anxiety and depression were impacting my overall life functioning, I began my journey to understanding my cognitive distortions. I started reading about all-or-nothing thinking, which was one of the cognitive distortions I engaged in. All-or-nothing thinking is a form of black-and-white thinking. The way individuals deal with their emotions, feelings, and people is impaired because they can't understand the nuances of others' actions or emotions. People who engage in all-or-nothing thinking have difficulty managing their reactions to certain events. In turn, they have a difficult time seeing the gray in life.

Another cognitive behavior distortion that I struggled with throughout my grieving process was called catastrophizing. Due to my debilitating undiagnosed anxiety disorder, I always thought the worst. My mind would race 24/7 with irrational thoughts. No matter how slim the odds of me dying or getting in a horrific car accident were, I had constant worry. If you have ever seen the movie *Chicken*

Little, you would see Chicken Little engage in a lot of catastrophizing behaviors throughout the movie to the point that when he was trying to tell the truth, no one would believe him. Understanding your irrational thoughts is extremely important to your grieving process.

Another cognitive distortion that many of us engage in is called discounting the positive. When we are grieving, it is difficult to see the world in a positive light. The joy in life, as maybe we had once seen it, no longer exists. There is nothing that we do in life that is good enough. This same mentality exists for those people around us. There is nothing that they do that is good enough for us. Hence, this distortion often impacts our relationships.

Think about it—if you don't feel positive about yourself and you feel absolutely inadequate, your view of people is skewed. Lastly, it is important to understand that cognitive distortions hinder us from thinking clearly. If you recognize this, then getting through the grieving process will be much easier.

Chapter Twenty-Two

Faith and Fortune

I remember a saying that I often heard growing up in my family: "Where there's a will, there's a way." As a child, I had no idea what it meant. It was not until later in life, when I faced adversity, that I would say this phrase. Being inquisitive, I looked up the meaning of the words and came to find out that this proverb dates back to the 1600s (Grammarist). It basically means if we are determined enough to do something in our lives, we will figure out a way to make it happen regardless of obstacles.

Where there's a will, there's a way, and so let our journey begin! I wholeheartedly live my life by this inspirational proverb. However, determination alone is not enough to overcome obstacles. From my experience, having faith in something bigger than myself helped me to overcome obstacles. I would never lie if someone asked me whether I have ever lost my faith along the way. I lost all faith in humanity. I felt lost in my own life with no direction. I began to question everything I was raised to believe in. Many of these questions remained unanswered. While I don't believe that asking questions is a bad thing, I found myself obsessing over each one.

I began to lose sight of the here and now and got stuck in the past. That is the interesting part of the grieving process:

sometimes, we don't understand. Remember when I said that time seemed to stand still for me while others kept living their lives? Well, what I came to understand was that time was standing still for me because I was stuck. Literally stuck in my life with no purpose.

Having a sense of purpose was the one essential element my dad always wanted for me. As a young adolescent, I distinctly remember a conversation that I had with my dad about my career path. I began talking to him about the possibility of becoming an attorney and defending those people who could not afford representation.

My dad was a realist and would so eloquently tell it like it was to all his children, but on this particular day, something changed about him. With excitement in his eyes and emotion in his voice, he said, "Becky, you are capable of great things in this lifetime! All you need is to have a little faith in yourself!

You are wise beyond your years and intelligent enough to do whatever it is you set your mind to!"

I have held onto that conversation for thirty-one years since his death, cherishing every word. Yes, my faith has been tested, but I realized a few years ago that, without faith, who was I? Without faith, how could I achieve great things in this lifetime? But most importantly, without faith, I would be letting my dad down because he was a man of deep conviction and faith.

Every night, as I go to bed, I am thankful for my beautiful family and my life. And every morning when I wake up, I feel fortunate. I understand that each of us believes in something different, and that is what makes the world such a fascinating place to live. I can assure you that having faith in something greater than yourself will bring an amazing amount of good fortune.

What is good fortune? To me, it is waking up each morning and knowing that I am making a positive difference in the world. It is watching my three beautiful children contribute to the world, and it is knowing in my heart that I have made my dad proud! Fortune is not about the amount of money we have; it's about the way we give back to one another. It is about being selfless and looking past our own needs to make a positive impact on those less fortunate. There is no greater fortune in this world than doing something greater than yourself!

Chapter Twenty-Three

The Road Less Traveled

I n life, we often hear about taking the road less traveled, especially during times of adversity. At least for me, I have heard that saying several times throughout my life. I have to admit that I have never been a risk-taker, let alone someone who strays from the road I was already on. Therefore, it terrified me to veer off the road, no pun intended. At some point in my life, I decided to take a chance on something different and embrace the road less traveled. It was an absolutely beautiful day when I set out to find a new adventure. I decided to take a long drive with absolutely no plan in mind. For me, that was a huge deal because I had planned out everything in my life.

I found myself pulling over to admire a beautiful park with a walking path that seemed to go on for eternity. As I began to walk, I was consumed with thoughts of my father, the legacy he left behind, and whether he truly knew the impact he had on his family and friends. I wondered if he ever realized his overall worth in his lifetime or if he ever thought about it. But most importantly, I wondered if he knew how much he was loved and respected by those people who knew him.

Unbeknownst to me, the first person I came to meet during my walk was Gene, who was my dad's supervisor at his place of employment. My dad's relationship with Gene went far beyond that of employee and supervisor. They became great friends, and soon, our families would be close friends. I am not surprised Gene was the first person to greet me on my walk.

Gene and I walked and talked for what felt like an eternity. He spoke of my dad with such admiration and love. Like my dad, Gene was a man of few words, but when he spoke, there was power and wisdom in every word he used. During our time together, Gene spoke highly of my father, explaining the intense stress he was under as a tool and die maker.

He stated, "Becky, your father had the hardest work ethic and would stay as long as it took to get the job done. He was dedicated to his place of employment. Often, your dad would get frustrated with the lack of effort other colleagues had while on the job. He could not understand the lack of their work ethic."

Gene explained that my father was a wonderful employee and a dedicated family man. He described my dad as an introvert when describing how he dealt with stress. My dad did not have a way to deal with stress besides smoking, which, in my opinion, is not an effective way to cope with life stressors.

Gene continued, "I have never established friendships with any of my employees, but your father was the exception to the rule. When I used to talk with your dad, I began to notice the similarities we had in life, our families being the most important to us. Your dad did his best to leave work on time to see all of your softball games. He never wanted to miss watching you play. He took great joy in seeing you at your best! Your father worried about his sons and what career path they would end up on. He felt that there was a lot of uncertainty going on in each of their lives. When he would speak of you, he stated that he wasn't worried about you and that you would be just fine. He stated that you were a driven human being, and he knew that you would be successful in life."

I talked to Gene about the irony of what he said about my dad not being worried about me. For decades after his death, I wondered if my dad worried about me and my future. I know that his time on earth was cut short and did not unfold as he had anticipated. I know that there was more he wanted to teach me in life.

I felt a sense of solace while talking about my dad with Gene. Gene told me that he believed my father's purpose in life revolved around his family. My dad frequently expressed to Gene his desire for his children to have a better life than he did growing up. My father believed in the idea that each generation should strive for more than the previous one, and that was what he did.

As our walk was coming to an end, Gene spoke about my dad's legacy as a tool and die maker. He stated that when my dad died, the entire tool and die plant where he worked closed temporarily. People were shocked about his sudden death. He stated that my dad was well respected and had so much more to offer to the trade.

As I walked down the road, I began to think about what Gene told me about my dad. He had so much more to offer to his career and family, but his life was cut short. After our walk, I sat down for a while to think about our conversation. All I could think about was Gene stating that my dad never worried about me. He knew in his heart that I would be fine in life. If only I had known this thirty-one years ago when he died. I still worry about a lot in my life, but knowing that my father did not worry about me brings some solace to me.

I began to walk down the road, and I stumbled upon a beautiful patch of purple flowers where a hummingbird lay. My father loved hummingbirds, just like I did. Hummingbirds always brought me to a peaceful place in my life. As I stood there admiring the scenery, I felt a poke on my shoulder. I turned around to find Mike, my dad's best friend, behind me. I gave him a huge hug and told him it had been a long time since seeing him.

Mike and I began to reminisce about my dad and all of the good times that our families had together. Mike told me that my dad loved his family so much and that all he ever wanted was for his three children to have a better life than he had growing up. He said that he was really proud of all three of his children and all of our accomplishments.

Mike described my dad as a perfectionist when it came to his career. In addition, he told me that my dad took on a side job on his weekends to financially support all of us. However, my dad really enjoyed making and fixing things. He was always tinkering, as Mike would say. My dad made the most beautiful clock in downtown LaGrange, Illinois. Mike told me that the look on my dad's face when he finally completed the clock was priceless.

Mike stated, "Your dad was his own worst critic and never felt like anything he did was perfect enough. But when he saw that clock, you could see by the look on his face how proud he was of his work. For the first time in his life, your dad looked absolutely elated in his creation. Your father was my best friend, and I considered him a brother. The day he died, I lost a piece of myself. There has not been a day that has gone by that I have not thought of him."

As I was finishing up my walk for the day, I heard someone yell, "Becky!" I knew that voice all too well. It was my mom. She was not much of a walker, so we found a bench and sat down. She asked me how my walk was and if I was doing all right. My mom was not much of a talker, so for her to ask me how I was doing meant the world to me. What I forgot to mention was that when I ventured down the road less traveled, it was the anniversary of my dad's death, Friday, November 13th. It was the first time I had been out on that date in several years. My mom knew how big it was for me to leave the house and came to find me. We sat for a while, reminiscing about my dad.

My mom stated, "I feel your dad's main purpose in his life was to provide for his family. He wanted the best life for all of us, a better life than he had growing up. He always said that he wanted his children to grow up to be well-rounded and successful human beings in life. Your dad was the best provider to me and to you and your brothers. I would also tell you that he chose a difficult profession. He enjoyed what he did as a tool and die maker, but he placed a tremendous amount of stress on himself. You could say he was a bit of a perfectionist. I see a lot of the same qualities in you, Becky. This is why I have always preached to you to take care of yourself. Your family is more important than anything that you might do in your career. A job is a job. There will always be someone to replace you. Being a mother and a wife is one of the most important jobs that you will ever have in your lifetime."

During this conversation, I sat in amazement at my mom and her wisdom. Never once did she feel sorry for herself or blame anyone for the way her life turned out. I am sure, in a sense, she had questions about why her husband died so young, but it did not keep her from moving on in life. She moved on at her own pace and took care of her three children. Being able to reach outside my comfort zone on this particular day and take the road less traveled brought me such great joy, and it allowed me to reflect on my life after the loss.

Chapter Twenty-Four

Finding the Meaning of Life After Loss

I spent what felt like an eternity walking the road less traveled, speaking with people who loved my father dearly. It allowed me to learn more about my father's life; it was amazing to me how much I did not know about him. Through the stories of other people, I was now able to see him as a well-rounded human being who was passionate about his family and his job.

As I reflected on the information that was shared with me, it made me happy to know how much faith my dad had in my future. Gene mentioned to me that my dad never worried about my future. He had all the confidence in the world that I would be all right. There was a part of me that wished I had known this information decades ago.

After my dad died, I lost all faith in humanity and questioned my purpose. However, I began to realize the irony of life! If I hadn't talked to Gene about my father, I would have never discovered this information. Knowing it renewed my faith and enabled me to recreate myself!

Choosing the road less traveled led me to discover more meaning in my life after experiencing loss. It allowed me to find clarity in my mind and hope in my heart. We begin questioning just about everything in our lives when someone dies. I believe that this part of the grieving process is inevitable. For many of us, our loved ones signified a huge part of our lives, bringing happiness, love, frustration, stress, or simple friendship; they left a lasting impression on us. Regardless of whether their impact was good or bad, their death has affected us. So, how do we find our purpose in life? How do we move on when life stands still? I wish I could say that I had the magic answers, but for each person, the journey looks different.

My own personal journey to find a deeper meaning in life after loss guided me toward writing. I focused on writing inspirational proverbs to get me through the dark moments in my life. Finding hope in writing something inspirational became an outlet for clearer thinking. I spent a lot of time alone, reflecting on my father's life and, ultimately, his death.

It was during my darkest moments that writing and exercising both my mind and body brought me clarity and solace. Most importantly, I often felt closest to my dad while walking or running and being out in nature.

Please don't get me wrong. The death of a loved one leaves a permanent void in one's life, but it is up to us to find ways to take care of ourselves. I knew in my heart that my dad wanted me to go on with life, no matter how difficult it might be.

Once I was able to begin getting through a day and find some clarity, I started asking myself what my dad would want me to do with my life. I began reflecting not only on my current state of mind but also on my future—something I had not been able to do for years after his death. It was at that point that I decided to become my father's "living legacy," carrying on where he left off in his own life. I would pay it forward to those around me, just as he did for me!

So, as you go through your own grieving process, allow yourself time to grieve at your own pace. Remember your purpose in your life. Your loved one would not want you to forget your purpose. Find your meaning in life again, no matter how difficult it might be! On your difficult days, force yourself to get out of bed and do something that makes you feel content. Put one foot in front of the other even when you feel like life is standing still. I promise you, one day, you will see that life is not standing still; it is waiting for you to find a new meaning in your own journey.

Chapter Twenty-Five

Embracing Life

I t is at your darkest moments in life that you must find your purpose. Without a sense of purpose, it is difficult to navigate this world.

First and foremost, in order to embrace life after loss, you have to be honest with yourself and others about how you are feeling. There will be good and bad days. Do your best to surround yourself with people who love you. Please know that there is no shame in having more bad days than good at certain times in your life. The anniversary of your loved one's death, birthdays, holidays, and precious memories that you shared will be challenging to get through, but allow yourself to face the roller coaster of emotions.

Secondly, rid yourself of any guilt that you might have throughout your life. Your loved one would want you to go on in life and be happy. Moving forward in life after a tragedy is unbearable, but your loved one would want you to embrace the life you have and make a difference in the world! There is no amount of guilt that is good for you; guilt only stunts your life's purpose.

Thirdly, after the death of a loved one, it is natural to find ourselves bargaining internally. It is our way of coping, hoping somehow to bring our loved one back. If only I had spent more time with him. If only I had called more or visited more. If I hadn't argued with him, then maybe, just maybe, he would not have died.

Ultimately, these thoughts often plague us, hindering our ability to fully embrace the present. Wishing won't bring our loved ones back, but what I can say is that moving forward and remembering them helps us confront our grief and slowly move on. I have said for years that I will never forget the day I learned about my father's death; that memory will remain vivid in my head forever. However, with time, we learn how to cope with the loss and find ways to get through each day.

Lastly, find a purpose in this lifetime that makes you want to get up every day and embrace life! It doesn't have to be a huge purpose; it can be something that gives you hope for yourself. Each person's purpose in life varies, and that's a good thing because if we all had the same purpose in life, it would be an absolutely boring world to live in. Be proud of your purpose, and never let anyone tell you that it is insignificant. Know that a loved one is watching from afar, beaming with pride.

My purpose will always be to help those around me and to be with them during their darkest moments. I shared that our experiences, whether good or bad, have a deeper meaning in life. I feel it's my purpose to help others understand the importance of reflecting on their experiences. Our experiences mold us into who we are and influence how we live on this earth. Please understand that there will be times in life when it feels like the bad outweighs the good. However, it is up to us to find the silver lining in our own lives! Just as my father told me decades ago, even in the darkest moments, seek out the silver lining and reach deep within yourself to find that intrinsic happiness, no matter how difficult it may seem.

Once I slowly found the silver lining in my own life, I transcended through the grieving process and began to see life a little clearer. I realized there was more to life than denial, bargaining, depression, anger, and resentment. I am not going to lie—learning to embrace life again was truly difficult because there was a piece of me that did not believe I deserved it. Frankly, I was terrified to embrace life because, in the back of my head, I always thought something bad was going to happen. It was not until I had my three beautiful children that I intrinsically and passionately began embracing life again!

It's hard to imagine what my life was like before having my children, but one thing is certain: I support and love them just as my father did for me growing up. They have given me a sense of purpose greater than anything I could have imagined. Although I am extremely humble, my children have a way of teaching me more about humility. They have taught me to embrace the here and now and never look back, only forward! They have helped me to find my inner child again, something I lost sight of many years ago. They have taught me that it's all right to be silly and embrace life without fear.

I have not been able to embrace life for decades because I lived in constant fear. I feared failure, not being good enough for my friends and family, and ultimately, death. These three innocent children taught me that it was all right to simply live without regret and to be proud of who I am. I can wholeheartedly tell you that my wonderful children taught me to keep going, even during the challenging days of my life. Therefore, I had no choice but to get up and take care of them. Something that I was absolutely grateful to do each day.

Finding and embracing life is a life-long commitment for those of us who grieve; there is nothing easy about the journey, but I can say that I am a living testament that there is a light at the end of the tunnel.

Chapter Twenty-Six

Live, Love, Laugh

There is not enough emphasis that one can place on living an authentic life. Live life to the fullest, love deeply without regret, and laugh as much as you possibly can throughout your lifetime! We often forget about the simple principles in life when dealing with tragedy. We lose sight of caring for ourselves emotionally, physically, and spiritually. I found that I was guilty of this. Each day can look the same, so it is easy to forget to celebrate the little things in life. At times, life seems mundane; however, we have to find ways to relish each day that we are alive!

Try to find a way to live your best life after the loss of a loved one. I know that it is easier said than done, but it is possible if you believe. For many years, I was only going through the motions in life. I didn't feel much other than emotional pain and physical heartache. At some point, I woke up one day, and I said, "This is enough. I need to live again!" I began finding activities that made me happy, and I began reflecting on the deeper meaning of my life. Reflecting on the deeper meaning of our lives can be challenging as it requires authentic soul-searching.

My greatest fear in life was having a loved one die. After the death of my dad, I had a very difficult time sharing a piece of my heart with anyone, especially when it came to relationships.

There was a real fear that if I allowed myself to love someone, they would die just like my dad. Therefore, I would have to go through the same agony. In time, I learned how to love somewhat differently than before, but I allowed myself to love again. I have learned that loving others enriched me and gave me a deeper purpose in life. As you go through your own journey in life, don't forget to allow yourself to love authentically!

Last but not least, never forget to laugh! Laughter has saved me from some of the most challenging moments in my life. Finding people around you that lift you up is vital to living a happy life. We often take life so seriously that we forget to live in the here and now. Do your best to appreciate what you have and find humor even when life is not going the way you planned.

I found people I could always turn to for comfort. No matter what kind of day I had, I knew I could pick up the phone, and they would be there to make me laugh. So, no matter where you might be in the grieving process, find those people who bring laughter into your life!

Chapter Twenty-Seven

Never Say Goodbye, but Rather See Ya Later

There is a saying that I live by: "Never say goodbye, but rather see ya later." I believe it is important to convey this to all those I love. We are not saying goodbye but rather "See ya later." There is something so definitive about the word *goodbye*, almost as if we will never see each other again. Even when my dad died and they were closing the casket, I said, "See ya later, Dad." As difficult as it was, I knew deep down that I would see him again. It might take decades, but I found solace in knowing he would be waiting for me.

Even with my own children, I always say, "See ya later." They understand why I use this phrase instead of saying goodbye. Grief alters us, and it's the little things, like phrases, that help us get by. For me, these three little words bring comfort. So, think about the simple words in life that can ease your mind as you pave your own way. I certainly found solace in them!

My oldest daughter used to laugh at me and call me superstitious because of all my sayings and beliefs. One day, while driving her somewhere, she asked me why I was so superstitious. I sat quietly, trying to figure out a good way to answer her question because I wanted so much for her to have her own thoughts and beliefs. I did not want her to be swayed by the way I lived my life.

At times, being superstitious allowed me to promote a positive mental attitude. In those moments, my superstitions made me believe in something greater than myself. I was the person who wished on shooting stars and knocked on wood so nothing bad would happen to me. Let's not forget about me not leaving my house on Friday the 13th for years because I was terrified that something awful would happen to me. We all have our little quirks, but for me, my superstitious beliefs gave me hope and really defined who I was as a human being.

My daughter sat quietly listening to me with a sparkle in her eyes and a smirk on her face, and she said, "Mom, I would not have it any other way. Your quirks, your genuine love, your sense of humor, and your compassion for mankind are all that I need in my life."

With tears rolling down my face, I looked at her as she departed the car, and I said, "See ya later, my beautiful girl."

Chapter Twenty-Eight

Intelligence Versus Wisdom

For many years, I compared myself to people around me and wondered if I was intelligent enough to initiate and maintain conversations with them. I constantly wondered how they viewed me, and for a very long time, I struggled to maintain eye contact.

For some people, maintaining eye contact during conversations is difficult and can actually cause anxiety. This would be the case for me. These thoughts have been deeply ingrained in my mind and very difficult for me to let go of when conversing with people. To this day, when I have to speak in public, I experience major anxiety. I have racing thoughts going through my mind, wondering what the audience is thinking while I am talking. I am someone who prefers to be behind the scenes rather than in front of people.

It took a lot of self-reflection to realize that my insecurities stemmed from my childhood. Yes, that is right. Many of our insecurities are a direct result of our childhood. If we neglect to acknowledge our inner child and our past experiences, we will persist in resorting to the coping mechanisms we developed in childhood.

You might wonder what your inner child entails. According to Dr. Carl Jung, everyone has an "inner child" that influences many of our emotions in daily life, especially when we are unaware of it. Dr. Jung, an absolutely wise and renowned psychiatrist and psychoanalyst, explained that losing conscious awareness of your inner child means losing a part of yourself, making it difficult to regulate your emotions (VeryWellMind.Com).

The idea of the inner child in therapy is fascinating, especially when considering how it influences adult behavior, particularly during times of grief. As I reflected on my own journey, I attempted to listen to my own inner child, especially while navigating through my grief. In turn, this made me reflect back on my own childhood. We all encounter challenging family situations, some more than others. However, we have to understand that what we are raised to believe in can shape who we become.

I was raised in a traditional Italian family where I was the youngest of three children. I always felt that my brothers were smarter, stronger, and wiser than me. They knew more, they understood more, and frankly, they were physically stronger than me. In turn, I did not feel worthy. Frequently, I felt unheard, and at the end of the day, I questioned my place in my family. My thoughts were no one's fault, but they became my reality. I grew up extremely insecure about my intellect and my physical characteristics. I never felt pretty or smart enough, and overall, I felt uncomfortable in my own body. It was a lonely and emotional place to be in life.

What I never understood was my perception was my reality. The inner child and negative thoughts never go away if you don't listen. It existed deep within me until, one day, I began actively listening to myself and my self-defeating comments. If we don't search deep down within our souls to recognize that our perception may be distorted, our lives will ultimately be dysfunctional.

For decades, I confused intelligence with wisdom, but honestly, I began to examine the people in my life. What I realized is that the most intelligent people did not necessarily possess wisdom. So, what is the difference? We can determine that someone has average intellect if their IQ falls between 85 and 115. Furthermore, a standard score of 115 to 129 indicates mild giftedness. And anyone with an IQ over 130 signifies moderate giftedness. Additionally, we can consider an intelligent person as someone who is well-versed in their field of study.

Honestly, what does this all mean? Every day, I surround myself with highly intelligent people, but the inner child in me is no longer feeling insecure, not good enough, or afraid to sustain conversations with them. On the contrary, I have learned over time that a human being can have all of the intellect in the world, but without wisdom, what do they really have in their lives?

Wisdom is the ability to delve deep within your soul to understand your life circumstances. It is the ability to learn that with every personal struggle, there is a lesson to be learned. Wisdom is a mindset on how we experience the greater world. I believe, as cliché as it may sound, that there is a reason behind everything that has happened in my life. I believe there's a purpose behind encountering certain people at certain times in my life. I cherish every conversation that I have with people I cross paths with. Throughout my lifetime, I have learned that true wisdom evolves from having deep and meaningful conversations about life's challenges and crafting a vision for one's life that makes a positive impact on the world!

Chapter Twenty-Nine

The Long Road Home

I liken grief to a long, winding road that, at times, can be dangerous if you are not paying attention to the direction in which you are traveling. Just when you think you know which direction you are headed, you get lost and veer off another way.

Grief has a way of overconsuming our entire life, much like when we become preoccupied with our thoughts while driving. The next thing we know, we are lost. I humbly admit that I've veered off the road one too many times because my thoughts consumed me.

The long road home does not have to be negative. It can actually be a positive experience in our lives if we take the time to reflect on our grief and its impact on us. So, don't be afraid to take the long road home, but remember these five basic principles throughout your journey.

First principle: I will always remember a simple saying that my father raised me to believe in: "What doesn't kill you makes you stronger." I grew up listening to this saying, but I never understood it until the day he died and years after his death. If you dig deep down within yourself, you will find meaning to this phrase. Please understand that unpleasant experiences can define who we become in life. Remember, it is up to us to find the silver lining and become stronger and wiser from those experiences. I will never say this will be easy, but it is part of the long road home to healing.

Second principle: When you are faced with the death of a loved one, the vision you had for your life slowly dissipates. You lose sight of what was important in your life. Your purpose becomes obscured, and you begin to question yourself. I don't think we realize how important having a vision for ourselves truly is. The only vision I had in my life was to graduate from high school and achieve a Division I softball scholarship. I didn't want my parents to pay for my college tuition. In addition, I wanted to be the first female in my family to graduate from college, and I wanted to make my parents proud of me. My vision in life suddenly changed the day my father died. I lost direction, and I lost my vision for a while. I needed help from those around me to regain my vision and to see that everything that I worked for was waiting for me, but I had to believe it. I just needed to envision it, and I was able to do this with the support of my loved ones.

Third principle: The long road home does not have to be a journey alone. My journey home was not always easy, especially when I was by myself. There were times when I took someone along for the ride. I eventually learned throughout the grieving process that it was better to surround myself with people who loved me than to go through it by myself. Allow these people to be by your side, and don't be afraid to guide them through the process. The long road home doesn't have to be about talking. It could merely be about being together in silence or simply talking about life. I didn't need people to understand what I was going through in my life. Honestly, there were times in my life when I could not comprehend what my life had become. The beauty of your journey belongs solely to you, so make it a memorable one!

Fourth principle: Search deep within yourself to remember what you were once passionate about in your life. What did you love to do? What were your hobbies? What used to excite you? Go back to the person you were before the death and try to remember everything in your life that brought you pure happiness. Slowly navigate your way back into those events that you were passionate about doing in your life. I promise you, it is all right to feel excited and passionate about regaining your life!

Last but not least, principle five: Don't be afraid to let love into your life. Remember what I said in a previous chapter, it is better to have lived, loved, and lost than to have never loved at all. The day my father died, a piece of my heart died, and I forgot how to love. It took me decades to repair that part of my heart, but eventually, I did. I was able to find it within my heart to find love on a variety of different levels. I regained my love for the outdoors and nature. I found love again with a man who would love me regardless of all my quirks. Most importantly, my three beautiful children taught me about the importance of unconditional love and helped me to be less cautious when sharing my heart. They showed me the value of loving beyond limits, making my long journey home a memorable one!

Chapter Thirty

Living Legacy

I t has been thirty-one years since my father's death, but to me, it feels like just yesterday. Honestly, not a day has gone by without thoughts of him crossing my mind. For so many years, I have tried to make sense of his death. The only consolation for me is knowing that he did not suffer. He passed away in his sleep and was now free from the stress of the world. I have learned that when it is my time to depart from this world, I have no choice in the matter. So, I try to live my best life!

I am not going to lie—I have my good and bad days. But on those bad days, I try to ask myself: What would my dad want me to do? Would he want me to give up and feel sorry for myself, or would he want me to persevere in life? I know all too well that he would want me to persevere and make a difference in the world! Your loved one would want the same for you—live your life without regret, allow yourself to grieve properly, and always remember that your loved one would want you to live a fulfilling life!

This brings me to the final chapter of *For One More Wish*, a book about hope, love, and the enduring celebration of your departed loved one who may have left this earth physically but will forever reside in your heart. When you have challenging days, remember that you are your loved one's living legacy, and you will carry on where they left off. It might be your job to help with any unfinished business they may have had in their own life. It might be to love a little harder and live without regret. It might simply be to live your most authentic life and do good in the world!

Every day, I question my purpose in this lifetime. However, I reflect on this question in an effort to evolve as a human being. I ask myself if I am being the best mother to my three wonderful children, if I am a good wife, if I am making a difference in the lives of those students and their families whom I work with, and most importantly, if I am making an impact on the world.

I have always strived for perfection in my life, but after the death of my father, I began questioning the idea of perfection. Honestly, what do we get from trying to be perfect? In my humble opinion, I did not get a whole lot from trying to be perfect. If anything, I lost sight of what was important to me. So, surviving through the grieving process and living to talk about it has been one of my greatest achievements! The grieving process taught me that there was no such thing as perfection. On the contrary, I was absolutely imperfect throughout the entire process, and you know what? I came out of it even stronger!

Please know that we are all imperfect, living in an imperfect world, and no matter what, your loved one will always love you regardless of your imperfections. I have always told my children that if we lived in a perfect world, it would be absolutely boring. What makes the world interesting is our coexistence with one another, stemming from different backgrounds that shape our uniqueness.

I believe living through grief has made me a stronger human being, and it has allowed me to courageously tell my story to the world. I am proud to say that I am my father's living legacy, and I will vow until the day that I die to carry on where my beloved father left off. His life might have been cut short; however, I made a promise to myself to live a wonderful life and do good for the world, just like I know he would have done!

For the people who bravely wrote their own stories, I wish you much peace and love as you continue to embark on your own journey in life. I hope that writing your own story allowed you to heal in your own way, but most importantly, live your truth and never forget to carry on where your loved one left off!

Remember to cherish not just that special day you spent with your loved one but also the countless moments you can dream of in your mind. Though our loved ones may not be physically present, I believe they surround us every day of our lives!

It is up to us to find the signs and to look around for our loved one's presence. As I said, there is not a day that I don't look for signs of my father, whether it be our special song that plays on the radio or the hawk that circles my car as I drive to and from places. He is with me always and forever, and so is your loved one. Open your heart, and let your mind relax. You will find that signs appear all around you when you least expect them!

For those of you reading this book, please know that you are never alone in your own journey. There will be people along the way who will unexpectedly help you in your grieving process. Please understand that there is no timeframe for going through the grieving process, so don't put too much pressure on yourself. Allow yourself time to feel all the emotions that go along with your journey and be vulnerable enough to reach out for help if you need it.

In closing, I have learned throughout my life that I am tougher than I ever could have imagined. I have navigated through the most difficult times of my life and lived to talk about my experiences. Don't be afraid to talk about your experiences because what we go through in our lives teaches us valuable lessons and molds us into who we are toward the end of our lives.

I vowed to myself over three decades ago to dedicate my life's work to helping people cope with grief, not just because someone has died but because life throws all of us curve balls, and we have to be ready to swing no matter what happens! I hope that my life's work has made an impact on those people whom I have crossed paths with. And to the perfect strangers in my life who sat and listened to my story, all I can say is thank you!

Lastly, *For One More Wish* is a book about never forgetting that it is all right to make that wish upon a star to spend one more day with your loved one and to allow yourself to be vulnerable with them. Writing about my special day with my father was a cathartic experience, albeit an emotional roller coaster. However, at the end of this journey, I found my way home. Writing this book provided me with the closure that I desired in my life. My hope for anyone going through the grieving process is that they, too, find their way home one day and that they use their own journey to positively impact others and pay it forward to someone else. At last, please understand that each individual's grieving process is different as it should be. Allow yourself to set your grief free and understand that your loved one would not want you to be consumed by sorrow, but to live your life to the fullest.

With much peace and love,
Becky Cortesi-Caruso

About the Author

Becky Cortesi-Caruso has dedicated twenty-six years to being employed in public education. A former school social worker, she eventually made the leap of faith into school administration and is currently an Executive Director of Special Education.

Becky earned a Master's Degree in School Social Work from the University of Illinois in Urbana, Illinois, and another Master's Degree in School Administration and Leadership from Benedictine University in Lisle, Illinois.

She has devoted much of her career to assisting families in understanding the importance of special education law and advocating for students with special needs. She continues to be passionate about working with families and their children. In turn, Becky was selected by the Bill and Melinda Gates Foundation to attend the Center for Equity Learner Equity Conference where Executive Directors from all over the nation were invited.

Becky was inducted into the Lemont High School Athletic Hall of Fame where she was honored by her school community, friends, and family. This was a great honor to Becky as she was recognized for her athleticism at the highest level.

In addition to all of Becky's professional and personal accomplishments, she is most proud of being an author and a mother. She is happily married to her husband, Michael, and the proud mother of three children.

Becky and her entire family, including Charleigh, know the joy and inspiration that comes from exploring the world of adoption. They have chosen to share their story, *Chasing Charleigh: An Adoption Story Filled with Hope* and Love in hope that it will encourage others to take the same leap of faith they did and explore the complex beauty of adoption. Lastly, Becky tells a courageous and poignant story that features her daughter Charleigh in her second book entitled: *Beautifully Biracial: A Young Girl's Journey to Love Herself.* This book examines the deep impact that racial discourse has on her daughter and the lessons learned throughout her journey.

Becky is excited to announce the publication of her newest book entitled: *For One More Wish*, a poignant story about surviving the death of a loved one and the journey that all human beings transcend through.

Made in the USA
Middletown, DE
02 October 2024

61827815R00083